The Brutal Truth

by

Jonathan Harnisch

The Brutal Truth

Harnisch Productions LLC
In association with Babydude Press LLC
36 Mariquita Lane
Corrales, New Mexico 87048
United States of America

Jonathan Harnisch

ISBN-13: 978-1522920724

ISBN-10: 1522920722

Printed in the United States of America and the United Kingdom

First Edition

I am an artist, author, and filmmaker who lives with comorbid schizoaffective disorder, as well as a range of other mental health conditions. In *The Brutal Truth,* I reveal my schizophrenic world with all its terrors and wonders. The book offers a raw and candid glimpse into the rarely told and poorly understood reality of living with schizophrenia—where "the only place where my dreams become impossibilities is in my mind."

The Brutal Truth is a collection of essays that brings together material that was written for my online community dedicated to mental health. I have over 100,000 followers on Twitter, as well as a popular Facebook group dedicated to mental health advocacy. This 25,000 word volume is written for others living with severe mental health conditions, as well as general readers interested in understanding the nature of psychosis.

I am the author of the semi-fictional and semi-autobiographical novels, *Jonathan Harnisch: An Alibiography* and *Second Alibi: The Banality of Life*. I am also a controversial mental health advocate, podcast host, and filmmaker.

Table of Contents

Synopsis: The Brutal Truth

Jonathan Harnisch is an "artist, dreamer, man on a mission, and human being just like you." He is also "a deeply troubled and disturbed person," who lives with schizophrenia, bipolar disorder, post-traumatic stress disorder, and borderline personality disorder. He is committed to sharing his unique life online in order to help others.

Through a relentless, direct encounter with his schizophrenic self and thoughts, Harnisch offers a rare insight into this often misunderstood disorder. Extraordinarily, the message is one of resilience and hope, finding rare wisdom through enduring and learning to understand his psychotic episodes. Rather than retreating into his own troubles, Harnisch journeys inside himself in order to understand the humanity that he shares with others: "The strongest people are not those who show strength in front of the world but those who fight and win battles that others do not know anything about."

For all its fearless honesty, *The Brutal Truth* is throughout an affirmation of life. As Harnisch says, "I write and publish what I want and what I feel, no matter what mood or state of mind I am in, but I always do my best to keep things positive." After all, he knows that he is "a legitimate, loving, grateful, and spiritual human being who deserves to be loved and accepted and who deserves to make decisions, to make mistakes, and to be forgiven."

The Brutal Truth shows that it is by acknowledging the schizophrenic experience that we can come to understand and deal with it. Harnisch's essays offer daring descriptions of what it is like to live—moment upon moment—with schizophrenia. These essays are written to help others undergoing mental disorders. They will also help those who want to better understand what their loved ones are going through so that they can help them more effectively and more compassionately.

But these essays are not just for those affected by psychiatric disorders. All readers will feel enriched after spending time with Harnisch in this extraordinary and too often untold schizophrenic world. As Harnisch says, "We schizophrenics, through our psychosis—our delusions, our hallucinations, our reality—create or develop a story." Seldom has the schizophrenic story been told with such unflinching honesty and truth.

Outline: *The Brutal Truth*

The Brutal Truth consists of 13 essays that shed light on the day-to-day experience of living with schizophrenia.

I Have Schizophrenia, but Schizophrenia Does Not Have Me

Even though we all have our battles and our bad days, this does not mean that we have a bad life. Harnisch describes his realisation that the ultimate goal that he is striving for, as a person living with acute mental disorders, is independence. He refuses to be controlled by his illness.

The Brutal Truth: Where Am I?

Of the things you lose as a schizophrenic, it is the mind that you miss the most. Harnisch describes his search for solitude, walking away from life to find peace but being unable to escape the past or his day-to-day problems. The truth must be spoken, however savage that may be: "You do not want to feel what I feel."

Thanks

Here Harnisch thanks his readers, especially his online mental health advocacy community, which has proved to be his "trapeze net" on his schizophrenic flights.

Getting Through an Episode

Harnisch is an unemployed artist with "a life that, in terms of conventional reality, doesn't actually exist." And so he creates a "double self" made up of his delusions. This double self allows him to experience a reality that substitutes for the uncomfortable truths he prefers not to acknowledge. It allows him to *not* be himself.

If You Are Going Through Hell, Keep Going

If you hang in there long enough, things will change for the better. In Harnisch's case, a severe psychotic break was required for him to finally get the right help. Whatever our hand in life, we must discover our worth: "what we give to the world and what the world gives to us." Harnisch cannot escape schizophrenia, but he can make it his friend. By altering his perspective on suffering, he learns that even though he still struggles, he no longer suffers.

It's Coming to Get Me: The Voices of Paranoia

If you are afflicted with paranoia, you know, wholeheartedly, that these are *not* delusions. People *are* harassing you. People *are* jealous of you. By now, Harnisch is able to see that his paranoid beliefs are "only the schizophrenia," but "it's for damn sure the truth and as frightening as all hell."

Living with Psychosis: Living in Shame

Nothing is more terrifying than battling your own mind every day. Harnisch's accounts of his psychotic episodes are evidence of his resilience and ability to survive. But he asks people who don't understand the first thing about him and his delusional reality to stop expecting "normal" from him: "We all know it is never going to happen."

People with Depression Cannot "Snap Out of It"

It is difficult to be told that you "inspire" others so long as you remain depressed. Harnisch knows that he *will* get out of this depressed state. But it won't be right now. People with depression cannot "snap out of it." But they can know hope.

Addiction and Schizophrenia

Facing an addiction is a scary encounter with the self—especially if your reality is schizophrenic. Quitting smoking is a battle that Harnisch knows he must fight peacefully. He is a warrior and a survivor. He should be able to do this. It is a common enough struggle, but there is nothing common about how this feels.

The Delusional Thinking Process: To the Victor Go the Spoils

Harnisch describes his latest episode of delusion and paranoia, seeking to demystify what has happened in his mind so that he can learn how to cope even better next time. As he digs more deeply into "the vulnerabilities of psychosis," he discovers that his delusions are for the most part rooted in a grain of truth.

When Delusions Are Real: The Schizophrenic Experience

How can people diagnosed with psychotic disorders get people to believe their truths? After all, once you've been diagnosed as being psychotic, your credibility is never the same. Harnisch reveals what his illness has taken from him, including recognition for his accomplishments. He puts together pieces of the "shattered stained glass" of schizophrenia, attempting to describe what is usually dismissed as "indescribable." He explains the often mystical schizophrenic experience of reality, which those who seek to help them need to understand.

When Things Get Better

In this essay Harnisch calls for positivity, love, and gratitude even as he struggles "through the minefield—the deep darkness and confusion—that is schizophrenia." It is by embracing even our darkest experiences that we are able to strengthen ourselves for the journey.

Writing Therapy: Easy Does It

Harnisch describes the metamorphosis that led him from the pursuit of fame to using writing as therapyefield—the deep darkness and confusiofor his mind every day and is able to come to a clearer perspective on life. "We all have problems, but let's not kid ourselves! It's how we deal with them that makes the difference."

The Brutal Truth

by

Jonathan Harnisch

Introduction: Surviving and Thriving

I don't know what I'm doing anymore. I don't know what I want to see. My world used to be worth living for, but now it's hard enough just to be me.

Life is short, but it's also wide. So to my dear friends, fans, and readers, just for today, I'm done. I am done crying, fighting, and trying. I am just done. Ever feel this way? I sure do. But I feel I should be rewarded for my struggles and my pain. I will win. So my wish to all of you is that you never, ever, ever, give up! Don't you dare give up. Make a fucking plan and work for it, every single day, hour, minute, and moment.

If you want something badly enough, you'll find a way. If you don't, you'll find an excuse. There are only two options: Make progress or make excuses. No more fucking excuses! Excuses be gone! To quote Pope John Paul the Second: "An excuse is worse and more terrible than a lie, for an excuse is a lie guarded." Are excuses more important than your dreams? Live. Live life. Be happy.

Some days you have to say "screw it, I did what I could today" and just let go of all the stuff you wanted to do. Life is too short to be angry with yourself for being human. Your hardest times often lead to the greatest moments of your life. Keep the faith. It will all be worth it in the end. I am thankful for my struggle because otherwise I wouldn't have stumbled across my strength. You will survive through hard times. Just believe that things will work out.

I could go on and on, but I resist the temptation. Sometimes you have to hold on to your sanity. There are people that have achieved mastery by making you believe that you are the crazy one. Just hang in there. We are all survivors of something. We all have the scars to prove it! Just keep going. Just keep going. We've got the power! You can do it; we can all fucking do it.

I feel so passionate about this right now. I feel realistic and optimistic, all the while knowing that my moments, seconds, and hours bring change, all sorts of change. I think of turning this diatribe into a longer writing excise, perhaps a blog post or the beginning of my new book, *The Brutal Truth*—a book written as an affirmation of life. Keep calm, and breathe, one breath at a time, accepting, when you can, each battle, no matter how big or small, one step at a time. Take baby steps, if you will. Great times lie sparkling ahead.

Does my life preach louder than my writing? I hope so. However, realistically, sometimes it's hard to practice what I preach. I think this is common for many. Thank you for taking the time to read my rant of inspiration—my introduction. I am an author that mainly writes erotic and transgressive fiction, often with very disturbing clarity and embellished with addiction, fetish, lust, and love. My professional writing is known to use pornography as a narrative device. This has attracted much criticism, but I try to keep it real.

The bottom line for my literature is to inspire hope, inviting others to question themselves, their reality, and their sanity by sharing my complicated experiences as a result of my diagnosis with schizophrenia. My work has been considered brilliant, and I keep at it. My point in mentioning this is that I have a heart that speaks. I am who I am. That is for sure. Honest, brazen, and often uncensored—with a stream-of-thought style. I invite you, my readers, to allow the brutal truth to sink in. Take what you want and leave the rest. I write from pure passion at the moment and that will change naturally according to my fluctuating brain chemistry. I feel fucking inspired, determined, uncut, and raw.

Please understand we are all human beings. We all fuck, up, and we all have our triumphs. We overcome—even if sometimes there is no closure. I try to get by—today—just like everyone else. What is the truth, the brutal truth? What is the final answer to all life's dilemmas, to all our vacillations of mood, thought, and perception, to all our triumphs and losses? Jesus, I don't fucking know. I don't think anybody does. The invitation here is to question the truth yourself, over and over again. What about the grief, phlegm, delusion, reality, response, confusion, complications, and clarifications that we feel the need to explain in order to be understood? Or perhaps we don't feel the need to explain?

My desire is not to be understood. I can't even understand myself. Why is there be a need to be understood rather than just noticed, loved, hated, and rejected? Why can't we simply be seen as lost as we all are—failed and flawed? The brutal truth for me is, at times, a sense, perhaps an emotional sensation—feeling bankruptcy, the bankruptcy of mind, body, spirit, and soul. What is the purpose of life? What is its affirmation? What are these big questions, these inspiring quotes we find online, and these gimmicks that are seen and sold on TV? Who are these fake people, real people, fake friends, real friends, enemies, and supporters that show concern, blame, apologize, and excuse? I just don't know.

I would like to share something I wrote on my private Facebook page: "I don't post much on this personal page. I get scared. I lie. I use people, and I suffer. No, I struggle, not suffer. I deactivate my account only to come back. I get frustrated, angry, and mad. I'm crazy, by definition. I am mad. I'm schizophrenic, and I often don't enjoy the decline, but I took my morning medication a minute ago and put on Duran Duran—they are playing on my favorite music playlist real loud. 5:15 AM. I realize that no, I am not scared. I am fucking determined. I'm a badass motherfucker. I'm the 'King of Mental Illness.' I'm smart as hell. No, I am brilliant! I love myself. I have a good heart. I'm beautiful. I'm often miserable. I live life. I live. I survive. I win. I lose. I rule. I rock the mic. I love music. I'm not stopping. I'm writing, posting, and publishing what I want and what I wish. Even with typos if they happen. I'm posting my accomplishments. My stuff. I'm barely awake still, but I kick it. Can I kick it? Can I get over the past? Can I get over the loss of my friends here on Facebook and in life? No, probably not. I kick it good. I am Jonathan. I am a living, breathing person, I am a survivor, and I know it. For today, I am just trying to get by, and I am unable to choose between different courses of action and opinions. I continuously waver through all the storms and sunshine. I keep hope and faith alive. I am doing my best as always, for whatever that's worth. My existence in itself gives me a reason to love, survive, and thrive—overall. And that's enough for now."

—Jonathan Harnisch

I Have Schizophrenia, but Schizophrenia Does Not Have Me

My name is Jonathan Harnisch. I have schizophrenia with psychotic features, but schizophrenia and psychosis do not have me. I cannot distinguish what is real and what is not real. My thoughts, mood and behavior are altered, and they change frequently.

Sometimes I believe that I live in a psychiatric hospital and that my experience is worse than a hellish nightmare. At other times, I don't believe this. I see and interact with people who aren't there, and I battle through countless other extremely uncomfortable symptoms. I believe that my medical team is currently taking me off all my medication.

My overall goal online is to inspire hope and resilience as a survivor of severe trauma that has led to dissociative disorders and schizophrenia. However, I struggle, not suffer. I post and publish what I want and what I feel, no matter what mood or state of mind I am in. However, I always do my best to keep things positive. I admire people who keep as positive an attitude as they can. Even though we all have our battles and bad days, this simply does not mean that we have a bad life. A negative mind will never give you a positive life.

The world suffers greatly due to the silence of good people. Keep going! Keep hope and faith alive! Living with schizophrenia and, therefore, with a brain that from time to time doesn't work means that my life can become difficult. However, I keep moving ahead, as always, knowing deep down inside that I am a good person and that I am worthy of a good life. Given that I've been diagnosed with schizophrenia, bipolar disorder, post-traumatic stress disorder, borderline personality disorder, a brain injury, Tourette's syndrome, diabetes, anxiety, depression, a rare blood disease, dyslexia, and cancer, I am doing okay. At the end of the storm there is always a golden sky. Writing in general—and writing this piece in particular—helps me by enabling me to stay in the moment and to share my experiences publicly.

I have recently had several days completely to myself, which provided me, at first, with certain feelings of abandonment and more solitude than I would otherwise have wanted, alongside moments of agitation, frustration, and anxiety. These feelings have fluctuated with familiar and comfortable times spent with myself and with my two cats in my home in the guest house of my family's large property in a small village in New Mexico.

I would like to point out that prior to 2010 I was an extremely wealthy and successful person, which made my precise diagnoses with mental illnesses difficult, as I used to be able to just pay for anything I needed or wanted. This difficulty was increased because of my natural abilities, as I have always been known to be very smart and I have always taken some pride in being so. I have been able to write volumes about my past, but my goal now is to stay as grounded in the present as I am able to be. This is because a change has occurred in me, something perhaps bordering on the profound.

Yesterday, I watched a documentary film called *A Sister's Call* about a man with schizophrenia, who eventually gets better and better over the years. By the end of this film, I felt a change in myself. During my decline, I lost a great deal of what I had, much like the schizophrenic man portrayed in the movie. I was able to relate in quite a few ways, although I think that the changes in me actually first began years ago, when, as a boy, I would often read about schizophrenia and related conditions, as well as self-help material. I have come to realize what I had, what I have, and what I want so far as this pertains to my health, my lifestyle, and, yes, my life. Independence.

I have been and am still dependent on people, as well as tobacco and medication. I have lost a great deal of my cognitive abilities over the past few years—and a great deal more since earlier this year. I continue my journaling as usual, but I feel different, maybe better, maybe not. There is no cure for schizophrenia.

24

I have read about living independently. However, I have overlooked the benefits of being able to take care of myself as far as possible. Even this possibility never really crossed my mind. Maybe I just had to see this movie at this particular time. I am glad for once. I know what I want and perhaps what I might even need. Independence. I already have a job and a loving wife and people to help me.

I began to think about how financially lucky I had once been and how, when I lost that, I let my condition get the best of me. I think my illnesses and their unbelievably complex symptoms have given rise to blame and denial. It wasn't that I changed my thoughts, attitudes, and beliefs. Instead, these have changed and shifted inside me. That is how I now see it. Yesterday I started to plan as efficiently and as realistically as possible, given my limitations, fears, and emotional dysregulation. All in all, I'll see how it goes.

Some bumps have come up already, which is natural, and I'm just giving this independence thing a shot. However, I do have hope. Nothing unrealistic. I have felt a delicate—and relative—equilibrium over the past 24 hours. That is rare. We'll see how it goes. One day at a time and one step at a time. Easy does it.

Once again, I try to make a good day out of what has been, but I end up hidden inside the fog of schizophrenia and asociality. Asociality refers to the lack of motivation to engage in social interaction, or a preference for solitary activities. Poor social and vocational outcomes have long been observed in schizophrenia.

I do not like interpersonal relationships or schizophrenia. I prefer to be asocial. I know many people miss me. Everybody does. I often miss myself. I sit, as I conclude this right now, completely alone, alone in the dark.

My goal is to raise mental health awareness to put an end to the stigma and maltreatment that occur so often regarding those with mental illness and physical disabilities. I continue to keep hope and faith alive. I will move on. I will move on! Thank you for blessing me with your prayers and well-wishes. I sincerely appreciate you, God, and life. Keep fighting! Let those of us who suffer from or struggle with chronic mental health conditions remember that we might have schizophrenia or a mental illness but it doesn't have us. We cannot allow it to have us.

The Brutal Truth: Where Am I?

What do I mean by the brutal truth? I am not sure. I am just trying to get on with my own sordid and colorless life.

"I question how life is treating me; I should be asking how I am treating life." —Jonathan Harnisch, *Jonathan Harnisch: An Alibiography*

I respond one year later. Not well enough.

I cannot distinguish what is real and what is not real. My altered thoughts, mood, and behavior change frequently. Primeval, latent, core emotions volcano to the surface together with centeredness, tears, and elation all made visible as the result of a one-hour therapy session. Priceless.

Sometimes, perhaps most times, I feel that I don't know what's going on or that I don't care about anything. I am confused by my feelings because I'm not able to explain how I feel, except for the emptiness, and I feel that no one is there, even if they are, or that no one understands me anymore. It feels as if I have nothing to look forward to.

I'm a compulsive liar, but I don't understand why I do this. I create intriguing stories about myself—to the point that I can't even tell who I am anymore. I lie to feel better about myself. Once I realize I'm a spectacular person just the way I am, perhaps I will then stick to the truth. I do try to respect people, including myself—even if they maybe don't deserve it. My lack of respect does not reflect the other person's character; but it reflects mine. I miss the mark, sometimes out of frustration, wondering why it is "always me" who tries to be right. I feel that other people are wrong at times, but, at the end of the day, respect is better than lowering myself, even the tiniest bit. I'm better than that.

I just woke up from another nap, and I write down my scattered thoughts about emotional pain, even though I am in a state of complete confusion because of the disorder currently in my life. Of the things I've lost, I miss my mind the most, though it might—just might—return even if only for a second. I believe I have lost the battle with my mind, but I still carry on feeling complete in my solitude in this enterprise, which is where I want to be.

I want to be alone. It is the closest thing I can think of to pressing the pause button on life, especially on the relationships I have with other people. I am a bad person to my wife. My biggest fear has always been that eventually she will see me the way I see myself when I look in the mirror—as a complete stranger. I can't stop thinking that I'm saying goodbye to my sanity. I believe I have lost this war—perhaps a long time ago. My mind has always been a dark place and not somewhere I would want my worst enemy to be, but despite all these feelings, I still battle depression and man, I am tired.

I want to feel like me again because, for a long time now, I have felt like someone else. The old me disappears as I fall deeper and deeper into oblivion. I need to be alone without any more external drama or chaos. I do not know how to deal with this feeling, except through anger, disdain, or withdrawing completely. When I can, I try to keep up with my art because it has saved me.

For my good and the good of others around me, I believe I need to be alone—not to be lonely but to find in my free time enjoyments or interests that allow me to be myself. Otherwise, I serve no purpose and certainly no positive purpose. I don't think I was ever meant to be. I don't think I have ever served any purpose—except to communicate through my art, mainly my writing, and to share these feelings with those who are unable to share theirs. I have nothing else to lose. Sometimes, I feel the stress of everything in the world trying to claw into my mind, constantly and all at once, and I need something to help push me through life. Something like writing, or maybe music, or sometimes just sleeping and not participating.

I have miserable feelings inside me that I can't seem to control, though sometimes it feels as if I can. Continuously, I fail. I hurt people, causing anguish, wretchedness, and hatred. I feel that I cause the same in myself, and so I stand back. I no longer interact with people due to this bizarre conflict that I do not know how to handle. I continue to fight for my wife and stepchildren and my many pets—but not for myself, as, in reality, giving up is not an option. It never has been. So far, though, I have lost this fight. I walk away from day-to-day life because I want peace, but day-to-day life and my past keep following me.

I try not to argue with the people in my life, and I still hope for something. I just don't know what I'm hoping for—maybe peace of mind and no more distress or conflict. If I do pull through the chaos, it will be because I had to be my own hero, once again. It has to be that way because no one else can destroy me when I destroy myself—when the schizophrenia destroys me. Please just save me. Fix me. I have fought this battle more than once, and I have still not won. It creeps up on me and terrifies me to pieces.

That's enough. I am as honest as I can be. Love me, hate me, hurt me, or kill me; I will still keep going. I'm still here—just entirely confused about how to relate to other, real people. I am a mental health problem, not a person. I am schizophrenia. I am no longer a person, not anymore. I sit back and watch the world go on around me, and I am a failure. The only place where my dreams become impossibilities is in my mind. I can't see what is possible, even when that something is better than the hand of cards that has been dealt to me. The war against my mind exists in a continuous loop, and that is why I keep fighting, even if nobody is aware of it. I have been absent from the external world and lost my broken mind. Do we call this depression or schizophrenia? I call it war.

I will leave it at that for now because I know this will barely make sense to other people, though I could be wrong. I can't give up, and I won't give up. Given my conditions, I am doing okay.

I'm fine. I'm just not happy. I'd rather be honest than impressive.

This morning I wrote on a post-it note: "Dear Life, you suck!" I am feeling a little bit better and stronger now. I am still not fine; I am sad, sick, hurt, angry, mad, and disappointed. Still, do you know what? I don't think people understand how stressful it is to explain what's going on in your head when you don't even understand it yourself. I am not sure if I am feeling better or if I am just used to being sick.

I went on a spending spree last night, spending a little over $10,000. My inheritance? Stolen due to family conflicts over inheritance, medical, and other power-of-attorney rights. But I'll just put on a smile and move on. It will hurt, but I will survive. Sometimes I don't feel like living. I don't want to kill myself; I just want it all to stop or go away. I want to be calm. I want to be happy. I feel tired—the tiredness that sleep can't fix. Every so often, I hope to fall asleep and never wake up. I'm scared. I'm scared of people. I'm scared of doctors. I'm scared of disease. I'm scared of life. I'm scared to die. Most of all, I'm scared of me. All I need is the right medication, with side-effects that won't kill me or make me worse and doctors that will listen and care. I need family members that won't judge me and are willing to help me with my journey, and I need friends that try to understand. I need my bed, comfy pillows, a heating pad, blankets, a good night's rest, and, above all, a fucking cure. Things change.

Time passes.

It is my delusion that I must lie about how I feel at any given time. Whatever I am feeling is a delusion. My argument is twofold. #1: I have a very severe form of Schizophrenia Spectrum Syndrome and other psychotic disorders. #2: While I have my good days, I am a deeply troubled and disturbed person. My lack of clarity here is deliberate. Some say I am brave putting it ALL out there, good, bad, and indifferent. Nothing. My life is full of continuous questioning, rationalization, guilt, and anxiety. I am not a motivational speaker. That is not my job. Please understand. I am a deeply troubled and disturbed person. I only write when sleep-deprived or symptomatic. I never get writer's block. I never get sleep. I. I. I. Me. Me. Me. I write and publish what I want and what I feel, no matter what mood or state of mind I am in, but I always do my best to keep things positive. I miss the mark frequently.

Truth. I love those who speak from their core, expressing whatever it is they feel—every last feeling. I thank everyone that continues to stick around with me online. I have no friends in real life and no family. I engage in deep philosophical conversations with store clerks, where the turnaround is quick. I see them once or twice at the Quick Fix on Maple Street and then never again. I am a wandering prophet of sorts—an oddball, a weirdo, an eccentric, and an intricate, lyrically minded creation. A nutcase. I feel my best when I am writing out my shame, my narcissism, and my delinquency. My insanity. My delusion. My life. I built something, and they came. I get to the core. I lose. I am mad. I am real. I am the real deal, shameless and raw, brazen and careless. Genius. My moods change frequently, and I currently don't know how I feel. I settle for nothing less than the bitter and savagely violent, brutal truth. Beyond that, I am... nothing.

There is nothing. I look in the mirror and see a complete stranger. I apologize for my exuberance. No, wait. I don't apologize for my exuberance. I revel in it. I encourage you to take what you want and leave the rest. Considering my all-inclusive mental and physical health conditions, I am doing okay. I keep some hope as I decline overall.

Should I erase these words, which exhibit too much brutal truth, and embark on something altogether new—to avoid embarrassing my family, my wife, my so-called friends? Should I stop telling the truth, my truth, in order to gain approval and acknowledgment? I don't need a following. I need nothing. Nothing. You know what? Never mind. Never mind me. I am staying here, onward bound as usual. The door is always open for you to leave me.

I am angry and upset; I feel full of loss and yet full of life. I was once built strong and healthy, but I now seem to be disappearing right before my psycho, crazy, failing, and diseased eyes. I am disgusting, and I hate myself. Right now. I do not appreciate, much less accept this predefined life situation that I experience— nor do I forgive anybody for it. I am a wreck. But aren't we all in some way or another? I rather think that this is key and that is my truth. My feelings. Many of you are religious. I am not. I still take pleasure and pride in your commentary, even if I disagree. Life is short. Life goes on. That is the saddest part and perhaps the bitterest pill to swallow. Where am I? Trust me. You do not want to feel what I feel.

Thanks

First, hello, good day, good morning, and good afternoon everybody! I have so much more to say, and I will do so when it's time and when it happens, even if it might be nothing in particular. I am currently on my cell phone and am still not used to the Facebook app interface just yet, so my apologies for typos and grammar. Second, I invite you to take what you want and leave the rest. Third, I want to respond to those very few who have not been so kind to me on my Facebook page. That is fine, and I forgive you. I appreciate you and—in fact—I love you. You're welcome to unlike or leave my Facebook page, but I will not ban you.

I have been awake for four days straight now and working hard on many projects and on my fight with my very advanced health conditions. I think that we all as humans can relate to this in some way or another. I have only one goal for anything that I write, whether the books that people pay for or this kind of free material. The truth. I don't care about money. I don't need likes. I don't need followers. I don't need appreciation. However, I have to write. Love me, hate me, or simply leave me, I post only what I feel is the brutal truth, which includes negative posts as well as positive ones.

I could lose everything at the drop of a hat. I understand that I have things under control overall. I have the help of money from a very large estate that has been used to set up a private psychiatric hospital setting for me. I have the ability to afford that. That is something to be very grateful for.

Forgive me. I'm not upset with you. I've just been awake for a long time. I'm working on a great deal of things while manic. I have nothing to lose. I just want to thank you all for your likes and comments—especially your comments and messages supporting and encouraging me. You have all been in your own way a sincere and solid rock of support—what I like to call my trapeze net. I feel I can count on you. I'm not here to slander or to hate—nothing like that. If anything, I end up hating myself. I post what I want, how I feel, and what I believe in—literally whatever is going on in my life at any given current moment. It's off-the-cuff, rock and roll, raw and candid, and I am an open book.

I have nothing to lose when it comes down to it. Besides, I have already lost everything over and over again. I went from living in a $75 million house to being homeless. That is not a delusion. Go ahead and judge me, if you wish. I want to thank you all for everything that you have been doing for me. My Facebook page has been turning out so differently from what I otherwise would have expected. I used to be very active on Twitter. I lost a great deal, having been hacked not just once but twice. I can't even begin to talk about the about the hacking and what I have lost. I'm sorry. On Facebook, I tried to get back to everyone I could, and, honestly, I can't keep it up.

I want to thank you all for keeping up with me. We all live our own lives. We all live through our own battles. We all come through in the end, no matter what happens to us. OK? No matter what happens to us. Yes, I've been through a great deal. I continue to go through a great deal. When I say I have nothing to lose, I say it because that is why I know for a fact that I am able to post and write whatever I like—and that is exactly and precisely what I do. This has always been my goal since I began writing as a child—for example, my first book of 25 pages published when I was five-years old. My moods, my symptoms, myself, my sense of identity, if that makes sense—these change like a chameleon, coming back and forth, blah, blah, blah. Jonathan (me).

I could go on and on, but this is a post about being grateful to each and every one of you. I am voice texting this on my iPhone, but I hope it reaches the right people. I do really appreciate that the majority of you have stayed with me. I always feel the need to apologize. That's just me. I feel a bit aggressive right now, but what is going on is actually something passionate. I'm passionate about health. I'm passionate about recovery. I'm passionate about trying my best to get back my 30 lost years, as my life has been cut short due to certain physical issues that I don't post much about at all.

To be plain and simple, thanks to each and every one of you. To those of you who leave, I learned from you more than you might ever imagine. Thank you, guys, again. Enjoy the day. Onward bound!

P.S. I did some writing therapy to get through a rather psychotic morning. I intend to post some of it soon if I am able. My day is rather booked with meetings and doctor visits—just living through another day. There is, of course, more to come. This is all coming from your friend and partner in life online through thick and thin. Can I kick this? Yes I can. Overall. In the meantime, let each of us fight our own battles and try to save our own lives in one way or another. Let's keep doing this. What do you say?

Getting through an Episode

The curtain opens. I am Jonathan.

I have schizophrenia.

For me, schizophrenia is similar to what I have read about it. In the early material, from turn-of-the-century psychiatrists such as Kraepelin and Bleuler, there seems to be plenty of subgenres or comorbidities with this condition, which I have had since I was a boy. I believe my traumatic upbringing likely set off my illness—though it did not affect my sister, who was brought up in the same environment. A series of other, seemingly continuous, traumatic events in my adult life have created complications, as my doctor would call them. I experience manifestations of other mental health conditions ranging from autism to borderline personality disorder. My case, for lack of a better word, involves many symptomatic days and moments, which often cycle rapidly. For example, my moods can fluctuate up to 30 times per day, with concomitant autistic experiences and muscular manifestations and malfunctions. A significant number of the comorbidities that I suffer from create reactions to even the simplest things.

I battle through daily life. I experience confusion with electronic devices, which is a common symptom of schizophrenia. I may need to reply to an email, but I forget how to do so. Or I go to turn on my computer, but I forget how to find, much less press, the power button. At the opposite end, on another day, or even another hour, I am capable of solving advanced logic and mathematical problems. While I often forget the simplest things, I have a photographic memory.

Let me back up for a moment.

I am having an episode right now. Therefore, I am writing.

Schizophrenia might be considered an umbrella disorder, though I am not a doctor of any kind. I consider myself an unemployed artist with a botched trust fund and a life that, in terms of conventional reality, doesn't actually exist. And so I create delusions, or, in a way, a double self—not a multiple personality, which is one of the myths of schizophrenia. This double reality, despite all the chaotically misfiring neurons in my brain, helps me to have experiences that replace the uncomfortable truths or situations that I prefer not to have. To exist. To be not myself, though loved ones have told me that there is a core, an "oversoul," that is intact throughout my schizophrenic life.

My thought trailed off slightly as I was about to write down one last part of my episode, primarily consisting of paranoid thinking that I should keep on writing through my episode until I could break through it. That is what I do. I archive my writing. Often, when I am feeling symptomatic, I go back to the categorized and collected written words that I have been documenting since I was a boy. This helps me to see what has happened through my own point of view and to learn how to cope better the next time. I take my writing to my therapist, explaining what happened. I often raise with him how my life is remarkably synchronistic with my books. I wrote these so that I can know, so that I can understand, and so that I can keep going and move the hell onward—as I always do.

I always come back.

My intention for this essay was that it would perhaps be a chapter to be inserted in my literature, my books, my documentaries, my life, my art, and my reason. But that thought has now trailed off as well…

What I would like to do now is simple: take a ten-minute break.

Time goes on, with people coming in and out of my office and interacting with me—communicating. My goal now is to return to my laptop and recall the five minutes after my last break; I mean my cigarette break when I wrote the initial thought that trailed off. Things change. Holy cow, things change.

I am back.

But I can't stop now until I complete this piece. My three-act play. My opera, where I am not the conductor but where I would be, naturally, if I did not have schizophrenia. I was the violin section. I was beating the melodic tom-tom drum. I was the full orchestra performing live, both alone and with an audience. Together, all the musical instruments communicate with each other, creating a rusty fragmentation, if you will, communicating with me, at my core.

I'll take a break now, and I will recap how I got through this one, this brief setback, and the five minutes that changed everything.

I know I can recall what happened. And I will. I never intentionally abandon what I am doing at any moment. Again, I always move ahead. There is some sun after the storm. If I can stay on track, or if not, while I still play this out live, some might be able to see the stream of thought that is my specialty, as I present a typical day living with schizophrenia. And I'll call it a good day at this point. I can't lose what I already have. If I do, I will grab something else and run with that.

In summary, if I am able to (for thoughts still bombard my psyche, overlapping and wild), I will, and if not, I will just move the hell on. Let this go. I should have better things to do than to examine my day-to-day experiences with schizophrenia.

And you know what? Maybe I will.

However, I can't leave anyone hanging. The show is not over yet. The chips are not down. I will simply do my best to finish on the stage, close the curtain, and become the director, the switchboard operator in my head. I have nothing to lose now. I am at war but not in combat; I am now in reserve. So let's get to some meat, the heart of this, and some completion.

Something.

Anything.

It is all so confusing and stressful.

Stressful?

Damn right. But it fuels me. It fuels everything.

No matter what those five minutes involved—tears, a hardcore crying spell, re-centering a crooked picture on the wall, a can of soda, a smoke—cigarette smoke, mind you. Nothing more. I can laugh now. Maybe it doesn't matter. My brain chemistry changed, all on its own.

I am back again. I have returned once more from the portals to that deep descent into Wonderland. That is something I am used to. The sun is now out, at last, and at least for now. Until, well, we'll just see what comes next.

Roll credits. Insert title card: The End. Fade Out.*

*Amendment: There is no end. I walk off stage. The seats are empty. I am back in real life. Well, sort of. The story of my life with schizophrenia continues. The curtain draws shut.

If You Are Going Through Hell, Keep Going

I love inspirational quotes and sayings. Most are simply reminders of how we should live life. Of course, this is easier said than done, and I think that's why they seem to float around everywhere, from Facebook and Twitter to blogs.

No matter how challenging things are in life, keep going. Never give up or quit. There are no other realistic options. We are all pushed to our limits at times, and there may seem to be no way out, no reason to move on, and no solution to whatever it is that is causing us to go through hell. What remains is hope, faith, and belief, although hope, faith, and belief on their own often cannot fix the problems and challenges we all face as we journey through our life—but action will. Keep trying over and over again. Through action, we will likely, though not necessarily, find a solution. When you've tried everything you can, change your approach, your perspective, or your angle, and battle onward. Do whatever you can. Just don't stop. I think this is what is meant by the saying "If you're going through hell, keep going". Keep going, because if you hang in there long enough, ultimately, things can and often will change for the better.

When I was initially diagnosed with depression in 1994 at the age of 18, I was prescribed antidepressants, including the newest of the selective serotonin reuptake inhibitors (SSRIs). Unfortunately, the SSRIs triggered mania, and so, to combat this, I began to drink, which intensified my psychological instability and led to an addiction that I was finally able to overcome when I was 26. However, as difficult as the disorders have been, in many ways I have been blessed. Many call me a gifted artist, and I have frequently used my art to exorcise my demons of isolation and loneliness. In 1998, I dramatized these issues in my award-winning film *Ten Years*, which I wrote, produced, and directed while attending NYU's Tisch School of the Arts. In 2008, I once again dramatized the themes of isolation and loneliness in another award-winning film, *On the Bus*, which also explores the horrors and chaos of mental illness. Through the eyes of the main character, we see the uncontrollable, tumultuous symptoms of schizophrenia and post-traumatic stress disorder (PTSD) as brought on by a random act of violence.

However, a single act of violence rarely causes severe mental illness; current research indicates that mental illness is the result of a genetic predisposition combined with environmental factors. My case would seem to validate that research, as there is a history of mental illness in my family and I have suffered repeated trauma. Whatever the genesis, beginning in 2009 and culminating in the summer of 2010, I experienced a severe psychotic break that manifested in inappropriate violent outbursts and destructive behavior. Ultimately, however, this break brought me the help I needed, including a comprehensive psychological evaluation that provided me with an accurate diagnosis and the right medication.

Now psychologically stable, I invite others to witness my candid daily encounters with the symptoms of schizophrenia. I willingly and genuinely share my life through my literature, film productions, and iTunes podcasts. In the vein of prolific figures such as Elyn R. Saks, Kay Redfield Jamison, and liver Sacks. I illustrate my ongoing personal struggles with chronic mental illness, nurturing truth, acceptance, and community. My art, imagination, and various creative outlets are my catalyst for continuous resiliency and recovery. As I turn another engaging and uplifting page of my story, I hope to impact others positively through this publicized journey of how one individual copes with the perpetual whirlwind of schizophrenia and Tourette's syndrome.

The quote "If you're going through hell, keep going" is often attributed to Winston Churchill, though I have never come across any clear-cut citations. How can we apply this quote to mental illness and its associated stigma?

Let's cut to the chase and keep it simple: Don't give up. You are walking through what is or what seems like hell. Are you going to just sit there and suffer, or will you choose to keep going—to overcome? Take baby steps. If you're in a difficult situation, keep moving on to get out of it. Recall the quote: "Everything will be okay in the end. If it's not okay, it's not the end." This means that you should not stop going until you get all the way through and, therefore, out! You're in a bad situation? Plunge forward. Things get better.

Don't quit!

What if there is no way out? What if things don't get better? Maybe you've had a stroke. Maybe you have amyotrophic lateral sclerosis (ALS, or Lou Gehrig's disease) or Alzheimer's, where there is no improvement, only deterioration. Are you a victim? Change your approach, your perspective, your angle. Consider how far the famed theoretical physicist Stephen Hawking has come with ALS. Hold the course, and then things will get better. Life often gets worse before it can get better. Life can press your brake pedal. What is there to do? How are we to deal with it? Do you roll over and take what life throws at you, crying poor me? Do you stand up to life without fear?

Are you worrying that it's not going to be easy? Nothing worthwhile is. It's how you deal with things and overcome what life throws at you that matters; it's about finding your worth, who you are, and your place in the world—what you give to the world and what the world gives to you. There is joy and sorrow. It is about learning about life and how we deal with it. It means that if things are really bad and life seems hellish, you don't give up and stop trying. Keep battling on until things improve.

If you think about it, life itself means "Don't give up." You walk through what at times is or seems like hell. "Just sit there," says that voice in your head, that imp, "and suffer." I suggest you fight intrusive, self-sabotaging thinking. Keep going through it to get through it. When I find myself in a difficult situation, I do my best, as gently as I can, to keep moving forward. I may never get out of schizophrenia—rather, schizophrenia may never, in my lifetime, get out of me. I keep hope and faith alive. I always do my best, and sometimes I miss the mark completely, over and over again.

So many quotes and famous sayings from Henry Ford come to mind. I invite you to ponder this quote, although it might not seem relevant to my thesis in this essay: "My best friend is the one who brings out the best in me." Make schizophrenia or your mental health condition your friend. Befriend yourself, trust the universe, and allow the universe to trust you. Trust in your higher power or God, if you have one, or just the reasonable part of you, your core when the mental illness is stripped away. Be who you are. Make mistakes. Dance. Love. Dislike. Judge or be judged. We are all here just trying our best to get by, playing it by ear. Life is in real time. There is no dress rehearsal. Part of the reason I prefer writing over communicating verbally is that I can later rehearse my writing by editing while also following my number one rule of writing first drafts, which I often publish, without any censor.

I often describe my experience with schizophrenia as every neuron in my brain misfiring. It sounds devastating. It is devastating. But if and when I am able to change my angle and perspective on suffering, I find that I struggle but I don't suffer. And I keep going. Hell? Hell no!

Maybe you have schizophrenia dominating your life as I do. Maybe you have a mental illness or physical ailment. Or maybe you're a "normie," an average person living life diagnosis-free. We all have our issues. To quote one of my books, "We all have problems, but let's not kid ourselves: it's how we deal with them that makes the difference." I consider myself a still-recovering schizophrenic, an accomplished writer, producer, and musician who blogs and podcasts about mental illness, New Age ideas, and transgressive literature.

In closing, be kind to yourself and others. Everyone is fighting their own battles and many unspoken secret wars. I am grateful that my readers sometimes consider me one of those voices that is able to communicate what far too many cannot.

Keep on keeping on.

It's Coming to Get Me: The Voices of Paranoia

Paranoia: The word is there, no doubt, in the dictionary. But not the feeling.

Derived from the ancient Greek, 'paranoia' originally referred to a distracted mind. But distracted from what? The definition claims that the distraction is caused by false beliefs that someone is persecuting us. But if you or I are afflicted with paranoia, we know, wholeheartedly, that these are *not* delusions. People *are* harassing and persecuting us.

Who the hell are they? Why the hell are they following us? What the hell do they want?

We have become the target of a vast conspiracy stretching on invisible webs across the surface of the planet. It lives in the telephone wires, the cell towers, the papers, and even online—perhaps even inside the dictionary itself. It spills out of radios and, these days, my iPod. And the damn TV too. It nests in the hearts and minds of my family, friends, and loved ones.

And it's coming to get me.

There might be many reasons why they chose me and why they chose you. But we have—in fact—been chosen, you know? People are jealous of us. After all, we're smarter than "they" are. They are after our brilliant knowledge, our money, our ideas, our mind, and all the rest of our stuff. According to the dictionary, many of us paranoiacs have "feelings of grandiosity and omnipotence." But no book really understands, though there are some excellent ones out there, including: *Understanding Paranoia: A Guide for Professionals, Families, and Sufferers* by Martin Kantor; *Delusional Disorder: Paranoia and Related Illnesses* by Alistair Munro; and *Whispers: The Voices of Paranoia* by Ronald Siegel, the first page of which I have paraphrased slightly in this essay, adding my own take given my own voices and current experiences with this diabolical perplexity.

You and I really do possess remarkable talents. We are mathematicians—like "the Great John Nash!" Inventors (that would be me!). Prophets (you?). That's why we are all so attractive, inspired, and envied. There is nothing in life that we cannot accomplish.

I haven't slept in two days, and I currently fear a complete psychotic break from reality as a result of my life being its own thriller-movie conspiracy—of which I am, of course, the victim.

This is no freaking joke. At this point I am aware that my beliefs are "only the schizophrenia," but it's for damn sure the truth and as frightening as all hell. Stuck. Trapped. No way out. But I have to keep running and playing along. In code. Like an FBI agent. Like John Nash's character, as portrayed by Akiva Goldsman in *A Beautiful Mind*.

Let's raise awareness and figure out this perpetual labyrinth of chaos and deception before it becomes more than just seemingly so.

Some of the above has been paraphrased from my second novel, *Second Alibi: The Banality of Life* (2014).

Living with Psychosis: Living in Shame

Time passes so quickly these days as I come upon my 40th year. The prognosis of my schizophrenia spectrum disorder becomes clearer as my cognitive abilities decline.

Life is an intimate and somewhat private stage. By contrast, the Internet is a public and global stage that is written in ink, not pencil. There is a curtain that always remains open.

Time passes. Time goes... Where?

"I've always loved the night, when everyone else is asleep and the world is all mine. It's quiet and dark—the perfect time for creativity." —Jonathan Harnisch, *Porcelain Utopia*

I forget the rest. I just don't care anymore. But the sad part is I actually do.

Love me, hate me, hurt me, or kill me. I keep fighting.

In a recent review in *Foreword Reviews*—known as "THE indie books magazine"—of one of my novels, perhaps my legacy, *Jonathan Harnisch: An Alibiography*, Alex Franks, in an excellent critique, writes: "Mental illness is romanticized at points in the text, as well, which may leave some familiar with the realities with an unsavory taste. That's not to say the work isn't well written—it's carefully plotted with well-rendered characters, presented in a narrative that would appropriately be deemed 'schizophrenic.'" To romanticize, we must deal with an event in an idealized or unrealistic fashion; make something seem better or more appealing than it really is. I must have been having a good day when writing those "romanticized" parts. But, Jesus, sometimes I know of no other way to cope.

The illness sucks. Schizophrenia sucks. And right now I think I suck. I'm sick. I am very sick. I was simply taking a nap in the house, but my so-to-speak real life is fully delusional. All the negative stuff, as my psychiatrist reminds me every day, are hallucinations or delusions. I am turning into my own book in many respects, and I still do not accept my overall mental health condition, not being able to tell what is real and what is not real, while my thinking, behavior, and mood are altered. That in itself presents a large problem—most of my problems.

I will be around. I hope I will be working, not sleeping. I don't know. As the day continues, I will try my best for you because I trust you, and I think you know that I would like your thoughts on things at some point. I understand that many of the things I ask others to do are simply unrealistic or out of their jurisdiction, maybe. I just don't know how to wing it. I don't know what I'm saying. I have no clue, though life is just impossible. I have to have a plan. I can't make one. I have nothing. If you have a full hour until one o'clock, feel free to leave messages of any kind. I just have nothing to say. Blah, blah, blah...

Too many problems to discuss, and they change—with additions and deletions. For example, this morning. And then *not* later in the morning. And then now, which means it has changed three times already. I believe I am not real and that nothing is real, not even that thought. All I do is hurt people. I am often ashamed of myself, mostly when I am around other people in any way at all. And I think I'm brilliant, and I talk too much, and I don't talk at all. I'm a complete waste, a failure, a miserable miscreant, and then it changes back-and-forth, back-and-forth, back-and-forth. You can see I'm trying to communicate, and I just can't. Anyway I am safe. I am not suicidal. As usual, I'm sure many are concerned, though nobody is here or there. I don't care.

This has already taken me 40 minutes to write. It sounds scary, and sometimes it is. Sometimes it isn't. Everything is in black and white right now. I just don't care about a thing. I have no idea what is going on, if anything at all. I lie, I cheat, I steal, and I use people. I'm a goodhearted person, I am smart, I am a creative, I am successful, I am wealthy, and I have my good times. Simply, in three words: "I don't know." But somehow I seem to get through it.

The sad part is that I can't help it.

The curtain opens again.

"Oh no, not him again. Not Jonathan. Not Harnisch," a chorus of voices chants in lyrical beats and a rhythmic tempo in my head. It's perfect. It suits me fine and fittingly so. I am hidden. Hidden at his meticulously cluttered desk covered in piles of books sits a frozen, mysterious, mosaic-eyed man in a tattered brown-and-yellow plaid suit. His thick salt-and-pepper hair is shaggy and mussed, his face unshaven, and his demeanor disheveled. His name is Jonathan Harnisch. Oh, that is me again. I can't get away from myself. Already up all night and day, and onto something else. Something new. Something.

I invite you to take what you want and leave the rest, as with all my work for that matter. I must apologize in advance, for I am having a bit of an episode and feel bitter, groggy, and, I might add, narcissistic—deriving from no self-esteem, perhaps. I am once again out of bed and inspired. I think. We'll see if it comes across. That seems strange to me. My introduction. As my father would say, bizarre and odd, and perhaps it makes him look bad since he is a public figure. I am sorry, Pops. This is about me and perhaps about my readers.

I have no idea how this is coming out. Just write. If I lose a thought, I'll grab hold of something else and run with that. God bless my scattered thoughts. I am leaving them in this writing without revision. And now, the Great John Nash. I mean, Jonathan. Yes, that guy. The same person as last time. Different but the same. Strange. To begin with my first unavoidable non sequitur, since I can't seem to think straight without sleep. 72 hours now. People are strange. No I didn't say that. Someone else did, I think. "How was that for an introduction?" I ask myself, but I hear no response. I often do. But I have always believed that anyone, yes, anyone suffering from any type of mental illness is one badass mother f*er. Nothing is more terrifying than battling with your own mind every single day.

So, get ready for this. It may not be for the faint of heart. Once, when promoting one of my novels, I was asked about the comparison of my work to Alasdair Gray's 1982 book *Janine*—a challenging book about power and powerlessness, men and women, and masters and servants. In reply, I said that this sexploration of the politics of pornography has lost none of its power to shock. It is a searing portrait of male need and inadequacy, a theme also explored through the lonely sexual fantasies of the character in all my work and most of my real life.

I am not here to promote my work. I have simply been starting to see my entire life as entirely and seamlessly in sequence with the story of my otherwise fictionalized autobiography. How pretentious of me, a Dostoevsky would likely say in criticism. One of my literary heroes—in line with the stream of fragmented thought I'm known for. I am a failed husband, lover, and businessman. But I am hopeful that I can use my wildly eccentric mind and reality in my work—as my literary playground. The playground of an author and all-around artist, dreamer, man on a mission, and human being just like you who also suffers—like all of us, in one way or another. The author (oui, c'est moi, l'auteur, the third person) laughs as he writes this, but hey, we're all for sale in some way. But actually, I'm all over the place. I'm in my head, my imagination, and my moment—comfortable here (comfortable nowhere).

Have I already lost you? Awesome! Keep reading. I do what I do, as they say, and I change. All the time, often taking delight in the touchy topic of madness, for example, in this brand new, raw, brutally honest, and extremely palpable psychiatric thriller that is part fiction and part truth and is featured in *Publishers Weekly and Writer's Digest*, among other literary publications—by controversial mental health advocate, Jonathan Harnisch (*Jonathan Harnisch: An Alibiography* (2014); *Second Alibi: The Banality of Life* (2014); *Sex, Drugs, and Schizophrenia* (2014); *Living Colorful Beauty* (2015)).

Ah, another reality begins slipping in. I am aware, I think. Maybe? Possibly. Maybe it's me, maybe it's the mental illness, and maybe it's nothing. Random rules! Ah, an oxymoron! I love it. Another illogical non sequitur? How many? I think I have already lost track. I'm still finding myself. What is the sad part? That is what I wonder. By the end, will there be some sort of whimper or instead a bang that resonates? Bordering on brilliant, I love this. Mania. Sleep deprivation. Stuff. Myself. I admit it, I won't defend myself. I don't. Usually. I'd rather find reality, as, otherwise, it slips away—every day.

Lost. My lost thought. Lost? Yes. I talk to myself. Even in my writing, my jibber-jabber. The voice in my head is speaking to me now. I take dictation, as fragmented as it is: "You're nothing but a waling cliché." I won't argue with that. I think the voices often tell me the truth. I love my alter egos and my double self. You can find them in my *Alibi*: Ben, Georgie, Tom, Claudia, Heidi, Kelly, and so on. My friends.

Fragment. Should I reconsider or break the rules of grammar? I choose the latter. I finished school. I write how I want these days. I am Jonathan Harnisch, the fragmented stream-of-thought, delusional, self-stigmatizing, at times self-loathing, four-times #1 Amazon bestselling author and #1 writer of hot new releases under the subject of schizophrenia. He introduces his ("Yours?" asks Dr. C, in my throbbing, labyrinthine head), yes, my, debut novel. Perhaps my pièce de résistance, *Jonathan Harnisch: An Alibiography* is now being taught at university level for its inspired and vivid portrayal of a disturbed reality, which is sometimes disquieting and at other times harsh. And with real emotions! It is culture-bearing, brazen, and bordering on brilliant—bam! Here she is, for 10 bucks (US), with all royalties donated to charity through the Jonathan Harnisch Foundation. Boom!

And then there is *Lover in the Nobody*, where Ben Schreiber (voila, c'est moi, c'est Jonathan!) has Tourette's syndrome, which causes him to display uncontrollable tics and hops, stuttering and swearing inappropriately. Bullied throughout his school years, he can never form firm friendships, especially with women. He's simply incapable of happiness. In his late twenties, he plunges into a downward spiral of drug and alcohol abuse that culminates in an attempted bank robbery using a cell phone as a fake bomb. He is arrested and placed under psychiatric evaluation, where his psychiatrist, Dr. C, quickly sees that Ben's affliction is more than just Tourette's. Ben is not alone. Inside his head lives Georgie Gust, Ben's alter ego. Georgie is obsessed with his manipulative and extremely sexual next-door neighbor, Claudia Nesbitt, and shares a sadomasochistic relationship with her that is supported only by his obsession. Claudia has no love for Georgie, and while Ben desperately searches for someone, Claudia Nesbitt, the perfect woman, is able to provide him with the unconditional love that he never received as a boy. He finds it easier to retreat into his mind and to share George's sick obsession with the cruel and abusive Claudia than to deal with his real issues. Dr. C senses that Ben is suffering from some type of post-traumatic stress that occurred early in his childhood and that he is using Georgie as an escape whenever bad memories start to surface. It is up to Dr. C to help Ben face the buried terrors of his childhood so that he can finally let go of Georgie and reduce him to the literary character that writer Ben wants him to be. Alas, if you don't have this book in your library or classroom, what do you have? Get your copy now!

P.S. I never said I was "normal." I suffer and move on. I laugh and cry. I write it all out and never give up. Sending light and love, from me, Mr. J.

I'm lost. I don't know what to do with my life. I don't know what I'm doing anymore. I don't know what I want to see. My world used to be worth living, but now it's hard enough just to be me.

Those who have experienced psychosis are stigmatized in our society, and those with schizophrenia are highly attuned to stigma. I live with both, and my life is spent living in my own way within the comorbid schizophrenia spectrum—with medical support, psychiatric and therapeutic help, and the work I do on my own to battle the symptoms and episodes that I experience frequently as my illness falls deeper and deeper into a state of decline. I still have my good days and my bad days.

It is interesting for me to look back at these written accounts of the bouts I have had with myself and with schizophrenia—and how I seem to always get through them. To me, that shows resilience. I am proud of that.

Tonight I haven't slept, again, so here I am as usual. Symptomatic and sleep-deprived, using writing therapy as my tool—my lifeline. I often consider writing in itself as my life.

I think all in all it comes down to the fact that other people in my life have all the say in my life and that they have full control of my life, although as I write I realize that this is likely my illness speaking; it is my mind playing tricks on me. I do not have control of my own life, and frankly I do not want control of my life because my mind with schizophrenia feels all too often to determine everything. I won't settle for anything less than the brutal truth. I'm not excusing myself from this either.

I am a troubled man. I am not good. I burn bridges. I can't make my mind up about anything. I can love, but I cannot fall in love. I don't know how to trust. I make more mistakes than I should. I am always sorry, but I never change. I am afraid of letting anyone else in my life get too close to me. If you want to come into my life, the door is open. If you want to get out of my life, the door is open. I have just one request. Don't stand in the door and block the traffic.

Sometimes I see no other way than to let other people go. I remove them and erase them completely from my life because I believe they are toxic to me. If I can, I let them go. I remove them completely from my life and do my best not to feel guilty about it. I frequently feel I have no other choice but to them go because they take and take and leave me feeling empty. I let them go when I can because in the ocean of life, when all I am trying to do is stay afloat, they are the anchor that drowns me. Unfortunately, perhaps sadly, when I blame other people, I blame myself. I let go of myself. That is one of the brutal truths about me. I will only settle for the brutal truth. I must also admit in confession that sometimes I look into the mirror and see a complete stranger.

You don't want to be me.

Schizophrenia is a mental disorder often characterized by abnormal social behavior and a failure to recognize what is real. Common symptoms include false beliefs, unclear or confused thinking, auditory hallucinations, reduced social engagement and emotional expression, and lack of motivation.

The saying comes to mind: "People will hate you, rate you, shake you and break you. But how strong you stand is what makes you." This comes into my mind, penetrating my mind. I must stand. I must keep going. There is light at the end of the tunnel. It's the damn hallways in between that get in the way. The hallways keep me awake, as I try to find the door and try to keep hope and faith. I have it. I have this. I will never give up. Never, ever. Never say never. "Never!" I kick ass.

When given the choice between being right and being kind, choose kindness. People may not tell you how they feel about you, but they will always show you. Pay attention. Spread kindness. Be nice to those around you. If you can't think of anything nice to say, you're not thinking hard enough. Smile at others and start a piggy bank for a cause, keeping your spare change in the piggy bank. When it is full, donate it to a charity of your choice. A sincere smile is a very kind and meaningful way to make a positive difference in someone's day. Without using words, a smile says to a person, "Hi, I hope you have a nice day." Help a child learn. When you look back at your childhood, you can probably name several key people who taught you some of the most important things you know today. You too can be an influential force in a child's life by spending time helping him or her learn. Though it is a common courtesy to say "Bless you!" when someone sneezes, people rarely do so unless it is someone they know. The next time you hear or see someone sneeze, offer those kind words regardless of whether or not you know the person. And if you have a tissue on hand, offer that, too!

Beyond anything else, the hardest part is self-compassion. You need that to do anything for others. That seems to be the hardest part, but is the first step. Again, by default, when given the choice between being right and being kind, choose kindness. It will make a huge difference if you can pull it off, one of those easier-said-than-done ideas. I speak from experience.

Thank you for reading these thoughts, some of which I have read about from various sources online and in books about kindness. I behave in this way when I can, often going to homeless parks and giving out food from a restaurant whenever I can leave the house. I have been doing so for years and years, and I even wrote a chapter about this in *Alibiography*, my debut novel—the chapter entitled "Benevolent Georgie." Enjoy your morning, day, or evening, depending wherever you are in your neck of the woods.

There is more to come.

I find this closure quite amusing. At the same time, in all seriousness, one final thought: other people who don't understand the first thing about me and my delusional reality should stop expecting "normal" from me. We all know it is never going to happen.

I hope this leaves you with a little laugh, all the while gaining a glimpse into my madness in order to understand or possibly simply consider your own.

Love me or hate me: I continue delivering this discourse as the unconventional mental health advocate that I believe I am, with problems galore: schizoaffective disorder, Tourette's syndrome with Autistic spectrum disorders, and PTSD. And all the rest not otherwise specified. I'm still the same bad-ass author and Hollywood sage with more to come.

Until next time, or to quote Jerry Springer of all people, "Till next time, take care of yourselves and each other."

I am and will always be Jonathan Harnisch.

An Email from my Therapist

My therapist responded to some of my recent writing and therapy sessions. I publish him publically! He is a good man!

Hey Jonathan—thought I'd email you since it takes me so damn long to type those texts...

In regard to your thoughts on Drs. A, B, and C having control over you—I can see how it may look like that sometimes. I can tell you that on the occasions when you request one (or all) of us to stay away and give you space, there is often quite a lot of deliberation about how to best help you. We understand your symptoms can be confusing and lead to confusing messages... and so we're ok with that! But please try to understand that if you request we give you space, or not, and we don't get it right—it's not because anyone's trying to be disrespectful. It's simply because we want to do the right thing—and sometimes that isn't clear in the message.

I know in reality there are a lot of decisions that are made by other people—I believe overall in your best interest. I can't imagine how unnerving that can feel! I think the challenge is balancing what is likely best for you and your own true independence.

It sounds like you haven't been getting a lot of sleep—so, if you change your mind today and need to sleep, I perfectly understand!

People with Depression Cannot "Snap Out of It"

My moods change frequently, and I am currently depressed. There is nothing more depressing than suffering from depression and feeling sad. So, what's the point? Will it pass? No doubt. I forget what it's like to smile—and by this I mean for more than just a couple hours. I'm talking about now, not later. I forget what it's like to be a lovely or loving person, or whether I ever was such a person at all—a person of love, of goodness, of graciousness. I forget how it feels to truly live, much less how to live life to the fullest. I just exist. Right now, I simply exist, with my pulse and my breath and maybe some tears, if I can bring myself to let them roll down my face in a river, flooding the seas and the world as they escape. I try to get myself out of this mood. This life. This episode of depression. Sure, I'll return to normal. Sure. Still, I have temporarily lost the point of living a life— pretending to smile and laugh, or getting a joke every darn hour when there are people around me that only want to see me happy. Well, I am not happy, and overall I have not been happy for most of my life. I sometimes glamorize the past and even the present. It'll pass, but that's not the point. The point is how I feel *now*. The point is *right now*.

Yes, I know it will pass. I know people love me, but I do not currently know what that should feel like. I just can't remember. I feel so lost. Gone. Yet I continue, and therefore I "inspire," I'm often told, but I am still depressed. I am still in this chair, writing out this rubbish. It gets so overbearing. I'm not alone. I know that, but it feels and sounds so contrived and lackluster, so uninspiring, to me right now.

I pretend to be so damn nice and funny and charming for others, just for "them," so I don't lose a Facebook friend or whatever. Nevertheless, I have zero real-life friends. I'm not sure I ever had any. Well, maybe, sort of, but they probably felt sorry for me. Who cares? I don't know. I am not even *my own* friend. This has been true for most of my life. I got into a good school, which I didn't even belong in. I lived my former Hollywood life, which never did anything worthwhile for me. I exaggerate about how cool that time in my life was, way back, back in the day. Now, I can barely move. I can barely see. I've been here many times, so don't worry about me. Just send a hug, as if I'd ever feel any real hug; virtual hugs are probably better because there is no effort involved. No feeling. I can only barely feel.

This is why I write this kind of stuff. "Just keep writing," says that little voice in my head, "Get it all out, all that you can." Do it now. Now. Now. Now. Get me out of right now. Remind me of some clever quote or cliché, reminding me how they are just reminders over and over again of how hard it actually is for anyone to do, let go, or move on. It'll pass, it'll pass, and so on.

I pretend to live, pretending to *be myself*, as if that would ring true. "Oh, that's just your mental illness speaking," some say. Well, then I guess I am just one full bag of happiness, and I am over it. Did I snap out of it? Of course. And again, I *will* get out of this depressed state, just not now, and I will do it only to see it return. I am incapable of getting even one positive thought out, so I am sorry for not pretending right now, even for just a minute. Maybe I still am pretending. I am sick, twisted, and wrong. I don't belong.

Other people have it worse. I suppose I don't deserve or have the right to be depressed. I need to think about them. Poor them. Hate me. Sometimes I pretend to love the life I live. What's the point? As Faulkner said, the reason to live is basically to get ready to stay dead a long time. Okay, thanks, Mr. Faulkner.

Seriously, what is the point? Tell me about it, about how we are all just here winging it, trying to get by. I am not "getting by." I watch the clock and wait, and wait, and wait for tomorrow. Oh, how sad and pitiful. Get rid of this guy, this guy Jonathan. Hell, I can't even walk two feet without being right here with myself, as myself. There is no escape.

I only know hope; it's that same hope that seizes me and brings me back here, for now. Tell me the point, and I'll tell you why I am so damn me, but it doesn't mean I'm proud of this. Make me understand you, as I try to do the same. People with depression cannot "snap out of it." Until my next episode. Until next time.

Addiction and Schizophrenia

My name is Jonathan, and I am a tobacco addict. Life goes on without smoking, but for now I fight for life. I don't write off a thing. It feels like hell, but I know it is peace—and strength. Overall, the symptoms are temporary. So far. I am nowhere near the end of the addiction, but I am on my way.

Help! I am kicking the habit. They are not going away, these withdrawals. The nicotine and the smoke itself. The real hardcore heavy chain smoker and tobacco fiend. A friend of the enemy. I befriend my fear. My fear of not knocking this off my bucket list before the bucket has its first and perhaps last heart attack. Or cancer. Or chronic obstructive pulmonary disease.

The severity of depression. Jumbled thoughts. Life goes on. I need this. I need my life. I crave life. No false hopes. The real deal. Quit. Win. Stay in the now. Stay alive.

Mental illness and physical disabilities aside, there is my body. I forgot about my body. For decades. It finally hit me. Something more profound than life itself. No assumptions. No projections. I am still figuring it out. Some are the smoke. The habit. The destructive behavior and serious issues of smoke. It might now remove some of my other issues. Just no more puffs. Slow and long steps on this slow and legal suicide. I am stronger than my mind. I can deal with life. I just need to preserve it as lovingly as I can. If I had resolved this earlier, sure, different story. I didn't, but I am now.

I have been offline and on my way—in combat with my mind, my schizophrenia, but now also with my body, my sensations, my second nature, smoke. Heavy smoke. Smoking is easy. Death is inevitable. But smoke. All that I have needed has been to feel its effects. 100 clouds of smoke each day. 120 cigarettes.

I can deal with schizophrenia and with mental illness. I am ready to quit the smoke soon and to live with life. Life is hard enough. I had an epiphany. I couldn't even walk 100 steps to smoke without being out of breath. For 10 minutes. Years full of lies that I told myself. It was my second nature. I needed to smoke and drink caffeine. Smoking, and quitting smoking—this is a battle that I must fight peacefully. I am a warrior. A survivor. A realist. I am still trapped in the wringer, but I am doing it. I am quitting. I have been quitting.

I have been offline and in detox. A slow detox mixed with the detox from yesterday's psychotic episode from schizophrenia and the crazy mess it left behind. That was a symptom of life. I let it go. Just quit. Just do it. Commit to something not by doing but by not doing. These heavyweight headaches. All of it. And I haven't even kicked the habit 100%. Not yet.

I am, however, on my way. Well on my way. Five packs of the six per day. I tossed them. I gave the cigarettes to my medical team to dispense for me: one pack day. That is the plan. I have quit, of course, 30 times. Honestly quit. But I never had a plan. I never outline. I just do what I do, and I still smoke. 80 cigarettes fewer now. 20 to go—day by day. I am stronger than my mind. I am stronger than my depression, my anger, and my withdrawal symptoms from letting go of four-fifths of my everyday life—of my addiction to death by smoke.

How do I sound? Raspy. How does this writing therapy session help? Who cares? It helps. That is all. It helps. I have help from others, and I use electronic cigarettes and lozenges. Thoughts bombard my head, my psyche, and my mind. They erase and delete. They change. They return. They are just there. Time to live life is available. It's been waiting for me. Time hones in, creeping closer to death. I knock out another puff. Lord help me. I can almost hear Him saying. I have been here all this time. I was waiting for you. Flight of ideas, racing thoughts, and then they slow down. But they won't stop. There is no easy way for anything, anything worthwhile maybe.

It sounds easy to quit. Just don't do anything. Smoke? Then don't smoke. Sounds good. Easier said than done. I would light a cigarette now because I wouldn't care. So I choose to take a breath, not to take away ten breaths—because I care. Nicotine replacement. Every ache and pain that exists. I fight a private war. A common war. It doesn't feel common. It is worse than kicking crack cocaine. A war of fear. The object that I fear will soon vanish because I now know that I am stronger than my mind. I can and will defeat this. You are stronger than you think, and the strongest people are not those who show strength in front of the world but those who fight and win battles that others do not know anything about. Maybe they do. Maybe they don't.

I rid my body of fear, of addiction, of hatred, because that hatred is fear. I am battling fear. I recently wrote about how the world suffers greatly because of the silence of good people. I have been silent because I fight a private war, a war of fear, of addiction, and of life. The thing I fear will soon depart because I now know that I am stronger than my mind. I can and I will defeat this. As the fear lifts, a freedom I never knew will mesmerize me. I can see it now; I can see it already. I am ready. I am ready now.

Can you see my face, with its eyes that speak, that drip tears and sweat, draining out the chaos of phlegm, of disgust, screaming with pure energy? They circle around. They see. Sort of. Dyslexic, legally blind, bestselling author bull. No. I can't either. Cancer eats at me. I take the Dallas Buyer's Club route. I take in and absorb my religion, my creed. I readjust to a new and improved lifestyle that will benefit me medically and emotionally. Have I quit the smoking habit? No. I have not. On Thursday, no. Tuesday, no, I can't remember. Blame schizophrenia, blame confusion, blame nothing, and not myself. Creativity keeps me alive. Music too. I kicked the crack cocaine, PCP, and hard liquor a dozen years ago. That is mine. It's easy. I am aware of how it will be.

I used to be a non-smoker, a person who didn't reap his body and the people around him, nor his health, I mean, his life. 25 years ago? I couldn't fathom the thought of smoke. Schizophrenia and smoke. Schizophrenia and cigarettes. They often go hand in hand. I used that excuse. I heard quitting tobacco can be harder than kicking heroin. I was on everything, and I would eat drugs out of the toilet. That was how stinging and demanding the fear embraced me. It overcame me; rather, I let it. Five packs per day. Five tins of smokeless tobacco. Something like that. I'd just use and abuse, abuse myself, my mind, my body, my spirit, my world, myself, my self-esteem. My pride. I didn't know. I carried a case of bottled water and cases of caffeinated drinks to my office just to get through six o'clock in the morning. "I'm an artist, a bohemian. I am allowed to smoke." Old Hollywood is now long gone—a time when smoking was glamorous. It was cool—to me.

Now, looking back? Guess what? It's astounding now. Excuses. Walking with a case of bottled water, for 20 yards, on the flat flagstone. Five minutes pass. The phone rang. It was important. I.D. theft or something. Stupid stuff. I was out of breath. The case of water, and those 20 years—not on my mind. My lack of clarity here is deliberate. About what I mean by these 20 years. "Hi, I just came back from a rigorous run, you know, a quickie five-mile jog...." Former New England Champion, 1993. Semi-Pro in 1994. Graduation day. High school. I am cool. I lit my first cigarette, just celebrating with the others. I had just graduated from the best school in the country. Easy. One hour later, one pack. An addictive personality. I was an adult. An adult! Big time baby! Smacked with suicide, a failure, hospitalized, music saved me. I called 911. That was mental illness. Depression. That was 1995. That was LSD. The next day ecstasy, PCP, junk, booze, malt liquor, fake I.D. Liar, liar. A friend of mine, where has he gone? I loved me.

Next up at bat. Hospital. "You have schizophrenia. Here is your script." The head doc meant my script for medication—not for my life. I was set. I was rich. I paid for friends. I paid for everything with Ben Franklins to spare. $25,000 per day, nothing illegal, no criminal record, no STDs, just some guys' stuff, some promiscuity, some garbage. Some things burying inside me, with my body bearing the burden. Smoke. Caffeine, too, and smokeless tobacco. I knew how to pack that. To be cool. I didn't say it—I just rolled with it. I knew that cancer and death—all that comes later. I remain in the moment. I was sick. Bottomed out. Quit everything. Square one. Just cigarettes. Let me stay sober for a year and then I'll just knock out the smoke. Dip. My teeth are fine, for now. I am a good kisser. The best. Big, sweet, sick, pure ego.

Literary word jumble. To cope. On Day 3 or 4. Something like that. No, I didn't quit. Here it comes. I am doing it right. Right now. Getting help. More help. As much as I can get. I want to live and not die. Much less to die a painful death. Leaving others behind. Not many, but maybe more than I think. I have a plan. Have I a plan? Is this a joke? Tapering off. Starting with knocking out packs instantly, indeed, instantly. Is it hard? I'll write 1,000 pages next time to explain how hard it is. One pack left. Caffeine? My last two vices? That's all. Wait. Is that all? Yes. And I am already on my way. It is either swiping the smoke or letting my life go. Choice point. Keep going.

I am stronger than my mind. To be continued through Christmas at least, maybe not on paper but for the documentary I have been making to capture these times of change. It's nothing. Something just hit me. Maybe it was—what's it called? God? I can work with that. Stay in the now, just for today, stay in the now. Let this sink in. Stay aware. Scan the body, in the name of God, and for the life of me, the life that awaits, the freedom. For crying out loud, my body is wailing. Just relax. Just relax. Just relax. What lies ahead? It is miraculous. Freedom. I can choose. I can. I can. I can. I am still on board. Turbulence expected. I'll get there. I turn 40 soon. I need this. I have this. Just for today. Just for this bloody second. I march on. I continue to surprise myself every day. I am my hero sometimes. Often. Quitting smoke is my war, my body, my mind, my fear, my fuel, my life, and ultimately my death. But I am still around. Being silent doesn't necessarily mean being forgotten. Thank you for your support.

The Delusional Thinking Process: To the Victor Go the Spoils

In the old days of war, the winning army pretty much got to loot the countryside and take what they wanted—wealth, crops, women, whatever. These would be the spoils of victory. In a relatively civilized setting, we tend to use this term symbolically or metaphorically. The winner (the victor, the victorious one, the one who gets the victory) gets whatever benefits go with the actual winning of the title, prize, award, office, or event. These can be formal or informal. That is, they can be a designated part of the prize (a gold medal, a contract with an athletics equipment manufacturer), or they can just tag along with it (celebrity status, free gifts, media attention, a boost in the winner's love life).

I don't want to focus on the illness of schizophrenia when I don't need to, but I do want to note some things I learned as I came out of my latest episode of delusion and minor psychosis, where paranoia was the overarching element.

Early this morning, I am refreshed and out of any episodic states related to my illnesses. I'm now able to access what it was like, yesterday, when I blended back into this more normal life experience. I want to demystify what happened in my mind—in order to learn how to cope even better next time. I want to figure this whole darn craziness out. The more I grow, and grow more comfortable with this illness, the more I'm looking for answers, solutions, and understanding.

Shortly, I will start my day, meditate, have fun, and, in a couple of hours, attend my psychologist's appointment. Perhaps then I will edit part of one of my upcoming novels. I will stay off the computer for the most part, I hope. I hope! But now I am thinking about delusions, hallucinations, and paranoia.

It seems that hallucinations, delusions, and, in short, any psychotic feature can be labeled as:

- White/Black

- Good/Bad

- Good/Evil

- Jesus/Devil

- Christ/Antichrist

I think that I have had experience of several such categories. Usually, one scenario will stand out, although they will often in fact overlap. The scenarios include:

- Religion

- Grandiosity/Celebrities

- Aliens/Conspiracy/End of the World—Doom

I made some of these notes during my episode and also as I was coming out of it using my coping tools, of which I have many these days. I'm discovering that my delusions are for the most part rooted in some grain of truth. In a way, they would represent, were they to be mapped out, my entire worldview. The storyline would have, I believe, more back-story, subtext, metaphors, and symbols (to use terms from writing). As a writer, who knows about the craft, I think my knowledge helps me understand some of this schizophrenia material, and I am finding, although I am perhaps slightly biased, a correlation between writing theory and practice—starting with the idea that I am in general fascinated with stories.

Some kind of historical context (Jung's theories play a large part):

"To the victor go the spoils." The spoils of victory are the extra bonuses, perks, and treasure you get for winning. Killers will kill for money and power.

Think of this the other way around, as our schizophrenic realities will often distort: "To the spoils go the victor."

Let's amp that up to a more grandiose context: for example, war and global catastrophe.

People are out to get me (paranoia) for money, power, and status. I often believe that this is true.

Then there's the storyline. As a writer, I often distort the story element in my writing, warping time, place, settings, and characters. You can see this in my films (including *On the Bus*, *Wax*, and *Ten Years*) and in some of my novels.

Story, story, story. The schizophrenic storyline—the delusional thinking process—is a healing process. Processes. I believe that this is the root of it all—that the storylines for me (and I would think for most suffering with schizophrenic or psychotic disorders—or thought disorders) are personal, synchronistic, and overlapping. Symbols, mythology, and connections, even coincidences, take on a very deep and personal meaning, a very deep and personal context.

I'm again digging a bit deeper into the vulnerabilities of psychosis, now that I am not currently experiencing an episode. Although my heightened awareness or metacognition often lets me know if I am episodic, it does not always.

Symbolic stories. Someone's tattoo of a cross might make me think that he (or she) is God—then I might confess my sins to a complete stranger. However, if I am aware enough, these days I can usually keep this to myself and believe wholeheartedly that yes, indeed, this person with the tattoo is God, no doubt, but I'll just keep that secret to myself. This goes for any delusion. However, this then leaves me, and us, susceptible to actual theft or simply vulnerability, since if, and when, something of ours, or mine, is taken, stolen, I am really and truly wronged. I often feel trapped with my secret of knowing this but having to pass it off as: "Okay, this isn't real… if that man—the man with the cross tattoo—is probably not in fact God, then no, my pack of cigarettes was probably not stolen."

This is frightening because if I saw my house burning down, I would likely believe this was real. This particular symptom is a common one for me. However, I would probably not do a thing about it, especially while in fear and stress from the event that I am experiencing, real or not. If I did make a call, the police would come and I'd be locked up for being schizophrenic, for making a fake 911 call, and I'd be scared—with many reasons to be scared.

Please note that some of the above writing is taken from my second novel, *Second Alibi: The Banality of Life* (2014).

When Delusions Are Real: The Schizophrenic Experience

The point of this essay is to start a conversation about how those of us diagnosed with psychotic disorders can get people to believe our truths. After all, once you've been diagnosed as being psychotic, your credibility is never the same, even when you're speaking the truth.

I have a podcast on iTunes in which I reveal a lot about myself, and lately I've noticed how much these podcasts have been teaching me about what I've lost. This illness has taken a great deal from me, including my ability to gain recognition for my accomplishments.

What I'd like to do here is recognize some of these accomplishments, knowing that had my life been different, they could have been acknowledged in a more public arena. Knowing, too, that, because I have schizoaffective disorder that is characterized by delusional thinking, hallucinations, and mood fluctuations, even when I speak the truth, I am often dismissed and not believed, with my truths dismissed as mere delusions.

I want to acknowledge my accomplishments not only for myself but also for all you out there. For those of you who may or may not already be diagnosed with schizophrenia, bipolar disorder, or any other serious mental condition, whose truths, like mine, are so frequently dismissed as delusions. It upsets me even to write this, as I realize that those around me can—and do—categorize what I say as delusional, and I wonder if that also happens to you.

I'd like to begin by briefly mentioning that I was diagnosed with Tourette's at the age of 12, although, according to my mother, I had shown symptoms since I was two. I sometimes wonder whether I was even then showing signs of the psychosis that has plagued me for my entire adult life.

I was 18 when I had my first psychotic episode. It was Christmas Day, 1994. I was living in New York City and was admitted to Beth Israel, where I was given a number of tests—medical and psychological.

My toxicology report came up 100% clean, a clear indication that my psychosis was not drug-induced. My intake report by the ER doctor shows that I had a "loosening of association" and "pressured speech," both of which can indicate schizophrenia, schizoaffective disorder, or bipolar disorder with psychotic features. No wonder it took so long for me to get the right diagnosis; so many of the symptoms overlap.

However, I want to bring this back to delusion and truth—how people so frequently label your truths as delusional as soon as you've been diagnosed with a psychotic disorder. I will also discuss my condition's genesis and prognosis. I will then move onto those accomplishments for which I've never been truly recognized.

Serious mental illness, such as schizoaffective disorder, is believed to be caused first of all by a genetic predisposition to develop mental illness and second by environmental factors. In my family, I have a grandfather who seems to have been diagnosed with schizophrenia, according to old medical records that I recently found. In addition, I have two second cousins, both of whom have been publicly diagnosed with mental illness. So, I would definitely seem to be genetically predisposed to becoming mentally ill.

However, having this predisposition isn't enough. You also need certain environmental factors. What I've read in some of the literature is that mental illness can be compared to diabetes. A person may be genetically predisposed to develop diabetes, but if that person gets enough exercise and watches their sugar intake, then the diabetes may never take hold—it's the same with mental illness.

In my case, I had the predisposition, but I also underwent enough traumas (sexual, physical, and emotional abuse) and upheavals (such as my parents' divorce when I was young) for the illness to take hold. Boy, did it take hold.

Sometimes, though, people like my sister, who has a genetic predisposition plus environmental factors (my sister comes from the same family and has had the same kind of upheavals), do not become mentally ill. Nobody knows why.

Maybe, as my wife says, it's just the luck of the draw. She's kidding. At least about the luck part, because having mental illness isn't lucky, although we do have to keep laughing about it. Keep positive. You're never alone if you can laugh with someone about it.

As I've mentioned, I have schizoaffective disorder. Originally, though, I was diagnosed with depression. That was back in 1994, when I was 18. Over the next 10 years or so, I saw doctor after doctor, moving here and there, trying to find my place in the world. I made seven suicide attempts and had years of alcohol and drug abuse issues. My last suicide attempt was in 2001, and I was freed from my drug and alcohol addictions in early 2003. More than 12 years ago.

As I was getting off the drugs, a doctor diagnosed me with schizoaffective disorder, which basically means schizophrenia with a mood disorder thrown in, and, in my case, that mood disorder is bipolar with manic features. However, in 2005 and 2006 I saw another doctor who said that I did not have schizoaffective disorder. Instead, I had a personality disorder. The point is that getting the right diagnosis can be time-consuming and frustrating, but it is also necessary, as once I was "re- diagnosed" with schizoaffective disorder, I was able to get on the right medication. But that's a different story altogether.

I'm focusing here on being diagnosed with any type of mental illness that includes psychotic features that then make it almost impossible for people around you to believe your truths.

However, not only do I have the double whammy of a thought disorder coupled with a mood disorder, I also have Tourette's syndrome, which is considered severe since this usually tapers off in one's 20s but mine did not. I'm 39 now, so, along with the confusion I suffer and the mood fluctuations, I also tic and sometimes engage in coprolalia, which is involuntary swearing or yelling out racial epithets. A hard combination.

Added to the mix, I also seem to have aspects of obsessive compulsive disorder—I have to keep my computer arranged "just so"; Post-traumatic Stress Disorder (PTSD)—I frequently relive earlier traumas; attention deficit disorder—I can't focus on anything for any period of time; autism or Asperger's—like Temple Grandin, I may be smart, but I can't read social cues at all. All this makes it difficult to hang out and just be "one of the guys."

My current psychiatrist, Dr. C, who—unlike others—never hesitated to diagnose me, saw me when I was at my worst. I was in the middle of a psychotic episode. I was in the process of a divorce (my wife and I have since reconciled), and I had no money as my family had cut me off from my trust income. In the past, too many doctors had seen me when I did have money and was able to hire people to do what I could not—shopping, driving, and cleaning, for example. Because these doctors saw me when I could hire people, they all considered me to be too "high functioning" to have any form of schizophrenia.

As a result of being considered "high functioning," I was diagnosed for years as having a personality disorder. Some doctors thought I had borderline personality disorder (BPD); others thought I had a personality disorder not otherwise specified (NOS). Let me tell you, having the right diagnosis has turned things around at last. I'm now on the right medication. My wife and caregivers understand the nature of the illness and know some excellent ways of dealing with it and with me.

Although the illness will never go away, I do have hope that I'll continue to get the right treatment and that my life will continue to get better.

Now, the big one: What do you do when people assume your truths are delusions?

Let's start with just a little bit more background. At the last count, I have had approximately 30 rehab stints and hospitalizations. That's a lot. When you're hospitalized, especially involuntarily, people tend to dismiss everything you say as a symptom of your illness. I understand that, but I don't like it. It's hard when people don't believe you.

A couple of examples. I moved to Los Angeles in January 2001 because I wanted to be a Hollywood screenwriter. I was two days shy of my 25th birthday. I was a go-getter back then, a social butterfly, and found it easy to introduce myself to just about anyone. As a result, I met Joanna Cassidy, Dick Van Dyke, Robert Downey Jr., Mel Gibson, and others.

Then, as my drug and alcohol use spiraled out of control, I got myself into rehab. Since I had access to my trust fund, I could afford the rehab facilities where "celebrities" went, places such as Promises in Malibu. In these places, I met movie producers, writers, actors, musicians, and kids of celebrities. The point is, I met all these people, and some of them I befriended.

Because so many of the rehab facilities didn't help me stay off drugs and alcohol, a friend and I started our own facility, Wavelengths, which also catered to celebrities. Wavelengths took a more proactive approach to getting people off drugs and alcohol. If you ever saw the show *The Cleaner*, you'll have a good idea what I mean by "proactive." In fact, that show was based on the friend with whom I started Wavelengths, and, although I was never credited, I was the co-creator of the show.

But now, when I tell people about *The Cleaner* or knowing Chuck Lorre, Robert Downey Jr., or Mel Gibson, they smile blankly, nod their head, and dismiss what I say as a delusion. That's maddening—if you'll pardon the pun.

Another example. In the summer of 2010, I checked myself into a facility in Colorado so that I could get on the right meds and become re-stabilized. As I was being admitted as a patient with schizoaffective disorder, which is characterized by a thought disorder, including delusions, both my wife and my doctor spoke with the facility before I was admitted so that the doctors and social workers would know I wasn't delusional when I spoke about the people I knew.

My wife and doctor also let the facility know about my financial background, as I don't always look "rich." Lately, I like to dress in t-shirts and pajama bottoms. I like to keep my hair permed and wild, and I like to wear a beard. As a result, sometimes when I'm admitted, the staff person will write that I'm a little unkempt, and when I then start talking about the money I'm worth, the same staff person will flash a little, tight smile as if to say: "Of course, you are. And I have a Swiss bank account."

Those staff people don't always know that I can "tell" what they're thinking—I can see it on their faces—and they feel free to openly doubt my truth.

The reason I write is to share my story, and sometimes—I've got to admit—it's hard knowing that a lot of people won't believe me. I bring this up because I'm sure that those of you who read what I write must have as complicated a story as mine.

I am just spelling out some things—kind of "straight-from-the-heart" sharing with you all. My family, as I've mentioned, is rich and powerful. Maybe your family is not rich or powerful, but still I think you'll understand. Their money and their power helped make me who I am, just as your parents helped make you who you are. I'm not attacking anyone. I am simply telling the story of my life. I have earned the right to do that.

Come to think of it, though, maybe I never did have to "earn the right" to tell the story of my life. People have a right to their own stories and to tell these stories in their own voice, not anybody else's. This is my time. My story. Not my family's. I owe it to you to share a taste of the complexity of my life, so you'll understand the complexity of your own.

So, yes, my family is rich and powerful. That is not a delusion. You can look them up yourself. They are public people. Sometimes I think that because they are public people, they have had a hard time accepting me for who I am. I know they have had a hard time accepting my diagnosis. Really, I am not attacking them. Maybe they can't accept my diagnosis because they think it will reflect badly on them.

I haven't talked to my family in a few years. I wish I felt sad about that, but I can't. My family doesn't love me. Sometimes I think they might even hate me, as they cut off my money and they cut off contact with me.

But I'm getting sidetracked—what my wife calls "going off on a tangent." So I'll stop.

One area that has always been hard and that created a lot of misunderstanding in my family is my diagnosis. No one has ever accepted that I had the wrong diagnosis for years and that getting the right diagnosis has helped me move forward. Not that a diagnosis makes the illness easy, and, in many respects, a diagnosis is nothing but a label. However, with the right diagnosis (or label), you can get the right medication, the right therapy, and people—like caregivers—who know how to deal with you. The right diagnosis is a starting point that enables you to find out more about whatever "label" you have been tagged with—or might need to be tagged with.

In my case, I was "tagged with" BPD for years. On the one hand, that wasn't such a bad diagnosis. It meant that people wouldn't then label me as delusional. On the other hand, when people thought I had BPD, they accused me of lying, which brings me back to my family.

In the past, my family has told me to "snap out of it" and to "get my act together"—that I would then be "fine." You can't "snap out" of schizophrenia. You may get the symptoms under control, and you may even, like John Nash, seem to recover from the disorder, but you don't—and can't—"snap out of it." My family's belief that I was capable of getting my act together created a lot of tension between us. I use the past tense here because I don't know if they now believe my diagnosis. As I've mentioned, we've had no contact since January 2010, so I don't know what they believe.

In January of that year, my family cut me off and stripped me of any help. I had no gardeners and no driver (I no longer drive). I had nothing. Based on what they wrote to me at the time, they seemed to think that they should provide a little "tough love" (like you see on *Intervention*) and that I would then agree to get better.

I was never not agreeing to get better. Believe me, it's no fun having schizoaffective disorder. If your family or loved ones believe your diagnosis, you are that much farther ahead because they can then help.

I'm taking my own advice today and staying positive. When I think of all I have lost, I can get very depressed. At one time, I had editors, housekeepers, free travel, a huge inheritance, my trust funds, and lavish cars. I've been to the best schools in the country. I had public-figure parents and several celebrities in my extended family, some of whom have actually, quite publicly, been diagnosed with mental illnesses.

When I compare what I once had to what I now have, I can become depressed. I focus on the past and fail to appreciate the present. Taking my own advice to stay positive: I have three dogs, seven cats, and one bird. Now, some people might not think having so many animals is a positive, but I like walking through the house and all the time being followed by at least one of them. My animals are a positive.

Another positive: I no longer have diabetes. I have lost so much weight that my blood sugar is normal. I still take one of the diabetic meds because it can prevent diabetes—and also because my other meds can cause diabetes. But I am healthier than I was. No diabetes is another positive.

My wife is the third positive. We reconciled five years ago, and so far we are working things out and trying to help each other.

My work is the fourth positive. The schizoaffective disorder has really affected my thinking and my emotions, but it hasn't touched my creativity. I podcast, I write a journal, and I make music and movies. I have even sold a couple of songs on iTunes.

My memories are the fifth and final positive for today. Although my father and I had a falling out in 2009, that's his issue. He and I have had great, absolutely fantastic, times together, and I treasure the memories. When I focus only on these memories, I can stay positive.

For many reasons, I have had quite a few psychiatrists over the years. My current doctor—whom I call Dr. C—is the one that most recently diagnosed me as having schizoaffective disorder. When I went to see her the second or third time, I brought along five bookshelves' worth of my journals. My diaries. All my written documentation of madness—the faxes and emails that proved that 1,000 hours of film that I had shot had been stolen. That's it. I can't do anything about it. I have proof of a software development proposal I made when I was 15. I received a scholarship to business school, honors, and recognition. I was like John Nash except I was proposing software, not math. What I proposed would have been the first online shopping interface. But it got taken away, like everything. I have the proof—the actual documents. Real. These truths are mine. I have schizophrenia, and I have delusions, but I know, and my wife knows, and my close friends know, that these truths are real—not delusions.

I spent three years of my life developing a show for A&E Television. I have the proof. I save everything. Faxes to the producers. My point is that I have lived an incredible life and often, all too often, facts become so-called delusions to others, especially to those others who actually count, like medical professionals.

And it matters to me.

All this really matters to me. It means something very special to me because it is about me. It is from my perspective and only my perspective—the only perspective I know for sure. It is part of my story, or, as some might consider it, the "myth of that stupid Jonathan kid." I know who I am. And I think I know who my friends are. I know that I am a legitimate, loving, grateful, and spiritual human being who deserves to be loved and accepted and who deserves to make decisions, to make mistakes, and to be forgiven—to be myself. The real me. The Jonathan Harnisch who is not alone—who is loved. The Jonathan whose moods and behaviors might be a bit difficult to predict. A guy. A citizen, with schizophrenia and a full spectrum of mental maladies, who believes in some kind of higher power. He believes in himself. He tries, tries, and tries. He stays resilient and never gives up— and never even thinks of giving up. He struggles every single day as an adult still being abused. He has been abandoned and treated like waste—a mistake. He is manipulated. Jonathan Harnisch. A teacher and a student. A rich kid who used to ride up front with his limousine driver. He used to be a real asshole, often due to his drinking and drugging—and to his mimicking what he saw growing up among people that should have acted better but just didn't know how to protect him.

I have been in therapy since I was 9, and from the age of 12 I was "put away" on far too many medications, some of which I am still physically addicted to, some of which caused me to gain weight and to develop tardive dyskinesia (chronic muscle stiffness), and some of which I was actually allergic to, causing me to rage and increasing my tendency to drink alcohol. I chose what I did, regardless what the literature suggests or what certain medical studies indicate.

I am who I am, and I have my own story—my own version of my own story. It changes and adjusts on a constant basis. I've been closed up for so long. I am opening up. I am not being inappropriate. I don't need to be judged. But I will be judged. I don't need to worry about what others think of me. But I actually do care what they think.

I can't control other people. Come to think of it, I can't control what thoughts come into my head, just as I can't control which ones leave. So how can I control other people or their thoughts? How can anybody control the galaxy? How about the billions upon billions of existing galaxies or the billions of galaxies that have not yet even been discovered? That is what we are living with—within.

Even Jesus experienced the full gamut of the human emotion spectrum, having been so-called spirit in human form. He was killed for that, for being who he was—for being honest and sincere, and, essentially, for being real. His life was far from easy. The most enlightened beings in the history of mankind— Buddha, Jesus, Mother Teresa, Gandhi, Krishna, and the Dalai Lama—have struggled and suffered every single day of their lives. And they too, in a way, live within us all.

I want to let you know that you are not alone. You will never, ever be alone.

I am excited and determined to come to you, who are seeking— seeking something. Maybe you are just reading as you sit there at work, or maybe you are my family, checking to see how I am and if I'm "misbehaving." What I am is a disabled and, yes, a very troubled adult. But I am allowed to share my story. My life. I am safe.

I laugh now when I say this, but my wife is 24 years older than I am. And if and when she passes away before I do, or for any reason leaves me (I doubt she will—we seem to be doing very well together), I worry that I will be forced into a psychiatric institution back east, back near my family, when we don't even talk. I worry that it's inevitable.

I guess, in conclusion, my life is full of grandiosity. But I still have schizophrenia, and I still have people who seem to have a need to control me and yet want nothing to do with me. This fascinates me. Why do they still want that much to do with me?

A staff writer for a local news magazine wrote the following about me. It makes me feel so good. See! Things can change.

> Envision a blend of a mentally ill mind with unsurpassed resiliency and fiery intellect and your result would be the brilliant Jonathan Harnisch. An all-around artist, Jonathan writes fiction and screenplays, sketches, imagines, and creates. His most recent artistic endeavor is developing music, a newfound passion with visible and of course audible results already in the making. Produced filmmaker and published erotica author, Jonathan holds myriad accolades, and his works captivate the attention of those who experience it.

> Manic-toned scripts with parallel lives, masochistic tendencies in sexual escapades, and disturbing clarities embellished with addiction, fetish, lust, and love, are just a taste of themes found in Jonathan's transgressive literature. Conversely, his award-winning films capture the ironies of life, love, self-acceptance, tragedy, and fantasy. Jonathan's art evokes laughter and shock, elation and sadness, but overall forces you to step back and question your own version of reality.

> Scripts, screenplays, and schizophrenia are defining factors of Jonathan's life and reality—but surface labels are often incomplete. Jonathan is diagnosed with several

mental illnesses from schizoaffective disorder to Tourette's syndrome; playfully, he dubs himself the "King of Mental Illness." Despite daily symptomatic struggles and thoughts, Jonathan radiates an authentic, effervescent, and loving spirit. His resiliency emanates from the greatest lesson he's learned: laughter. His diagnoses and life experiences encourage him to laugh at reality as others see it. Wildly eccentric, open-minded, passionate, and driven, Jonathan has a feral imagination. His inherent traits transpose to his art, making his works some of the most original and thought provoking of modern day.

Jonathan is an alumnus of Choate Rosemary Hall. Subsequently, he attended NYU's Tisch School of the Arts where he studied film production and screenwriting under Gary Winick and David Irving. During his studies at NYU, he held internships under renowned producers Steven Haft and Ismail Merchant. He is best known for his short films, *On the Bus* and *Wax*, both of which boast countless awards, including five Indie Film Awards and three Accolade Awards, and *Ten Years*, which won the Best Short Film and Audience Award in the New York International Independent Film and Video Festival, to name a few.

Despite his impressive formal education and awarded honors, Jonathan is your normal, down-to-earth guy. Meditation, Duran Duran, vivid colors, Patrick Nagel prints, and rearranging furniture are some of his favorite things. Vices include cigarettes, Diet Coke, inappropriate swearing, and sausage and green chili pizza. He enjoys irony, planned spontaneity, redefining himself, and change. Jonathan lives with his beautiful wife, their three dogs, and seven cats in the unique desert village of Corrales, New Mexico.

What follows gives a glimpse into how I have been putting together some of the pieces of the otherwise "shattered stained glass" of schizophrenia, as I see it—from what I have read, heard, and simply believe.

My psychiatrist has often asked me to describe or explain my symptoms, and thus schizophrenia, and I usually do not know how to do so. I simply reply that it is all "indescribable."

Since then, I have been looking deeper into myself so that I am able, at minimum, to summarize at least a few of my experiences, past and present, in order to share with you too some of the complexity—demystified. I'd like to share some of my discoveries, as I find them, concerning my experiences, false perceptions, and schizophrenic psychosis. Hopefully, I'll succeed in maintaining simplicity so that others can benefit and perhaps understand this otherwise extremely complex disorder.

I have come to realize that thanks to my own self, my lovely wife (whom I've known for over six years now), my support team (medical doctors and friends), and even those who might be considered my enemies, I have been helped along the path to self-actualization and thus to self-understanding—to where I find myself today. I've been able to find some meaning in schizophrenia, which helps me redefine how I see myself and how the symptoms of schizophrenia came to be—so that I can describe these without simply dismissing them as "indescribable."

Please forgive any terminology I might use incorrectly, as I am not a doctor. Also, I do have schizophrenia, so although I have stabilized (recovered, not been cured), I must still admit that I might get it wrong sometimes.

We schizophrenics, through our psychosis—our delusions, our hallucinations, our reality—create or develop a story, a storyline.

What is real has many universal implications. Some are extremely personal, symbolic, and moral. As we build the framework of our delusional reality, which tends to fade in and out, as with dreaming, it can all become very mystical. Our realities, which we may have had all our lives, can become delusional for mystical and magical reasons. So, for example, when we are psychotic, the television might seem to talk to us, or we might see and know Jesus—again, for reasons of a mystical or even religious nature. It becomes difficult for us then to realize that it is not necessarily real.

The further and further we are or are not drawn deeper into a full blown psychosis—it's just baffling, to say the least—the more it is complex and disorganized. However, we might believe wholeheartedly that our delusions are real and based on facts—facts that are not correct to others without the illness.

Many episodes, thoughts, and experiences combine, thus building up a storyline, which then becomes more intense and even fascinating and seductive, with more and more meaning as the delusional realities or events go on—as our lives go on. The meanings become "hidden" or disguised—our realities, in a way, hidden.

This illness can thus become very isolating because we have a whole different belief system about the entire world, especially when we are in a major psychotic episode. It can take years and years to arrive at this fully agitated state, but that is often how we schizophrenics will end up being diagnosed, just as an alcoholic usually "needs" to bottom out completely before getting help.

Through our perceptions, which change over time, we develop a new way of thinking that becomes very hard for us to disengage from. It is exactly like being on a constant LSD trip, every single day.

This is the bottom line, and, for me, this "acid trip" never stops, even when I recover. It is a matter of training and re-training our minds, through therapies like cognitive behavioral therapy (CBT), medications, treatments, and also a lot of training—mental training, which I do on my own, as well as in sessions with my doctor. I'm always checking things over and "reality checking." I also find it very helpful to have a friend or loved one do what I call "mediating my reality." I can, for example, ask my wife, who loves me deeply, to see if something is or is not what or how I might be perceiving it to be—from her there is perspective without the illness.

There is an element of losing what is called object permanence or object consistency—as my doctor in California once told me. The famous child psychologist Piaget discovered that, at a very young age, infants will forget about a toy they have been playing with if it disappears from their vision: for example, if a ball rolls out of sight or someone puts it underneath a blanket. However, at a certain age, that child will begin to look for that missing toy, and, finding it under the blanket, realize that it was in fact there the whole time. It was always there. Before that it had, to the infant, mystically gone away—disappeared from the world entirely.

That's what I mean by mystical. We lose object permanence, as something could, after all, just be a sensation rather than the fundamental reality one would have perhaps thought. We see this mysticism in most of our experiences. Yes, it fades in and out, but we basically feel that things, in general, usually happen for mystical reasons. This becomes a part of our belief system, which is pretty hard to change.

Enter the double bind, as, when object permanence is out of the picture, we can be caught in a contradiction, or a series of contradictions, due to cultural or moral as well as personal and universal reasons. We might, for example, in place of object permanence, experience a "multiple realities" effect, as if we were in several dimensions at one time—several realities. Based on how we grew up, at any given time a reality may slip into our mindset, and so, for example, we might behave like a racist even though our best friend is African American. It doesn't "make sense."

During my last psychotic episode early in 2010, I collected and even wore Nazi memorabilia, and yet I am half Jewish, on my mother's side, and handicapped. I also behaved as if I was a racist, even though my best friend is African American. We might want to save the world from global warming; however, in doing so we might pollute it and drive gasoline cars, on purpose, in order to save this world. My lack of clarity here is deliberate. Grandiosity, extreme thinking, and thus extreme behavior—with realities slipping in and out—are only a part of what baffles science and medicine. Different realities, slipping in, overlapping, and combining, make for an extremely difficult scenario to treat and understand from a scientific perspective.

Poetic thinking can also take over, and thus our symbolic and deep personal feelings are a huge part of how we schizophrenics think and reason. We might hallucinate about Jesus for a seemingly concrete reason, a very special reason.

When helping someone with schizophrenia, a good starting point is to remember that he or she thinks mostly through mystical concepts—the idea that everything happens for a deep reason, that everything has a very special meaning, and that everything is synchronistic. A schizophrenic is often a very traumatized and sensitive person living in a brutal world. That's where the help— the recovery—really starts to take place and healing begins.

We schizophrenics must learn, through counseling, to understand ourselves. We must participate in therapy to sort through our delusional thinking and get back as much of our accurate intuition as possible. We must take our medicine, and we must seek to have love and understanding in our lives. In this way, we might be able to reveal our secrets to someone we can trust, our secrets of trauma, day in and day out—and to do our best, resolving as much inner conflict as we can. Peace of mind is what we all want and need. It is my number one goal in life and always has been. It is what we all deserve.

Developing a new identity through our recovery is key in many ways. We must find our voice so that we can be heard and so that we can sort through our mystical, religious, and spiritual experiences and observations of reality. It is a matter of finding those people we can trust to help us define or redefine our reality.

I have that these days, especially through my wife and my doctors. I live with gratitude.

Just like diabetes, schizophrenia simply does not go away—not yet—for any of us. It's always there in the background. The "lifelong acid trip". I want to examine why and how we tend to cling to delusional thinking—why I cling not necessarily to a particular delusion but to this kind of thinking. It is "dimensional" for me. It is a grieving process for me. I am referring to missing my old Hollywood lifestyle—the content involved with that lifestyle of the rich and famous and the grandiose nature of the thinking itself. The celebrities I befriended when I lived and worked in Los Angeles, for example.

During the onset period of schizophrenic delusions and perceptions, we often begin with smaller-scale hallucinations. There is a root that is actually rational, wrapped inside a delusional outer layer. I think we can actually reach the schizophrenic while that individual is in a completely psychotic state—which often our doctors, caregivers, and loved ones fail to do—by understanding that everything the psychotic schizophrenic individual thinks happens in a synchronistic way.

It all starts with our loss of object permanence—that the one reality we once believed in has been replaced as a result of thoughts and events in our lives. There is a flow of realities, of things appearing and disappearing at the same time—not just the simple ball under the blanket, as the rules of both time and place also come into effect here: The time is now, and the place is grounded right here on earth. Let's call it an earth belief or thought. These thoughts and beliefs can, through the "schizophrenic lens," occur at essentially the same time. A waking dream, a constant LSD trip, real-life synchronicity (Carl Jung first coined the term "synchronicity"), and a more fluid mindset. If we are to think at the same level as a schizophrenic in order to reach him or her, we must think synchronistically.

If we are not stable enough or properly medicated, our dreams can actually become part of the same reality as reality itself. For example, my wife once asked me, "Jonathan, are you going to be recording an episode for your podcast today?" I had been planning on doing so, but I had not yet told my wife. I simply said, "Oh yes, I was actually thinking about it. It's been a while since the last one." Now, if I were in a more psychotic state, I might have (or, rather, the delusional process might have) started with my real-life fascination with Edgar Cayce and psychic ideas, my New Age books, and my meditation and interest in the Akashic field. I would therefore have concluded that my wife was secretly reading my mind or that she and what she said were mystically connected in some way—that she "knew something." My psychic experiences in the past would then have overlapped with my wife knowing something psychically, mystically, and symbolically, as well as with synchronicity—creating a deep and personal meaning. Add to that the paranoia that comes from her "reading my mind"—that she must be "God" because she knows I'm planning on recording my podcast today, even though I haven't told her this. The terrifying belief is now engrained, as we schizophrenics are to begin with often more sensitive with respect to the world—even being touched on the hand or the ear can create extreme fear for schizophrenics.

Synchronicity may have a little or some scientific evidence, at least theoretically. However, there are things that we cannot prove through science, such as the definition of time—or even God. In a state of schizophrenic psychosis, this overlap becomes compounded, as it builds up more intensely and thus perhaps takes over our entire belief system. My lack of clarity here is deliberate.

Perhaps there is a coherent way of explaining how we schizophrenics create our own reality, our delusional or schizophrenic reality, as I see it, through some of the things I have laid out so far. Please bear with me here.

I'll speak for myself, and my own experiences, although the end result is now something I can talk about and demystify rather than something I actually believe—thanks to the proper treatment, therapies, and support I now receive.

I'll first start with a collection of thoughts. Theoretically, let's say, for real:

> • In 2008, I made a film called *On the Bus* about mental illness.

> • Mel Gibson (an old friend from California) and I were first introduced to each other in 2001.

> • I listened to The Beach Boys. We'll assume that the music was playing in the car as Mel and I went for a drive, as we used to do, up in the hills of Malibu.

> • Mel Gibson is rich and famous.

Whether we are in a state of schizophrenic psychosis or not seems to be a matter of degree—depending on how psychotic we might or might not be and how much the psychotic part of our minds has taken hold. This is a matter of our abilities and the constantly fluctuating brain chemistry that we might—or perhaps might not—be able to filter through. It depends on whether we have been successful in redefining our delusional realities to a generally consistent state of well-being and peace of mind.

In a psychotic state, due to our hallucinatory thinking, the chemistry in my brain, our brains, is constantly misfiring, with the result that stimuli from the environment go to the wrong places in our brains. The effect is similar to putting our hand under cold water and feeling hot.

As a result of this schizophrenic thinking process, I would come up with a "composite sketch," if you will, a sort of "Frankenstein" version—a storyline that might be experienced as:

> • I knew Mel Gibson, and therefore I am famous. (Based on: Mel Gibson is famous and is rich.)

• Then—but at the same time—I am rich because I made a movie called *Ten Years*, and I am convinced it made me rich because Mel Gibson is rich, and I am famous because I made my movie and it won awards, and Mel Gibson did too. I must have met Mel Gibson because I made a movie, and he did too, and we are both rich and famous.

Time can in this way be altered—2008 comes before 2003. This might be a little hard to follow, but please bear with me here.

If I were asked to explain this while still psychotic, I'd say first that I am not mentally ill—I am simply psychic, rich, and famous. Besides, the Beach Boys were playing, and one of the Beach Boys has a mental illness, not me, but my film was about mental illness. Brian Wilson is rich and famous, and also an artist, so he was playing on the radio because both Mel and I were both artists and it was "meant to be" that he would be playing music for us because we were all connected through art, fame, and money.

Exhausting, isn't it? But this is actually how jumbled it can be for us and also for those witnessing us speaking and communicating. It's schizophrenia.

Let's assume that we got pulled over for speeding. Well, there is a police officer character in *On the Bus*, my movie. You see, grandiosity, both real and imagined, content and time inconsistencies, and now this character was in the movie, so, because we were all in the car, we were in the movie while in the car, so the police officer was playing her role—it all happened for a reason. And beyond that, paranoia might also slip in—the officer who pulled us over was male (not female), and in my movie she was female, so she was disguising herself in order to take our money and meet three famous people (even Brian Wilson on the radio).

Theoretically, this might suffice as a pseudo-case study, and yet in normal reality, for us schizophrenics, this type or process of thinking compounds itself and thus can become completely distorted.

Our friends and families start to think we're going crazy (in a way we are), and stigma arises, plus confusion. And so people say, "What the heck happened to this guy—he's speaking like a drug addict who has lost his mind. Where is all this coming from?"

We would all benefit from greater awareness of what schizophrenia is and how to know if someone we love might be predisposed to the illness (through family history, etc.). But this is what we who have schizophrenia usually experience early on, as the illness is progressing. We believe this thinking based on other facts that are disconnected, something we cannot see without appropriate help. Later, yes, we can also have this type of thinking while recovered or recovering, but we are able, hopefully, to be mindful enough to cope with it differently. Down the road, we can even do our own "reality checks" so that we do not talk about these things inappropriately in public. We can use "evidence", the hallmark of CBT, on our own in order to connect the disconnected parts of our thoughts—our reality. We can also do this with the support of family, loved ones, doctors, friends, and support groups that help us and love us enough to assist us in connecting the right pieces together and in explaining why they connect.

To conclude, I have not even mentioned the hearing of voices and hallucinations—everything from shadows to friends—and the hidden, traumatic, and paranoid features of schizophrenia of which we are often too afraid to speak. We might sound or behave cryptically, in code, with pressured speech and flights of ideas. Add to this the "zombie-like" features, the manic episodes, the muscle dystonia, and the side effects of the medication. And if we have turned to drugs—often just one hit of pot to quell the symptoms—yikes!

We're often too embarrassed to speak of our early experiences with schizophrenia or to say: "Yes, indeed, this is an extremely devastating and debilitating illness." I am so glad that I am at a place in my recovery. I do have my bad days. I haven't even slept during the last day—insomnia (technically, another symptom). But I am glad that I have been to this intoxicating wonderland and come back—just enough to be able to deliver this explanation, perhaps demystifying in a way that others can understand some of these processes that affect about 1% of the world's population.

Some of the above writing is paraphrased from my second novel, *Second Alibi: The Banality of Life* (2014).

When Things Get Better

"We all have problems, but let's not kid ourselves: it's how we deal with them that makes the difference. Don't let people make you feel bad or guilty for living your life. It is your life. Live it the way you want." —Anon

As a survivor of severe trauma that led to dissociative disorders and schizophrenia, I hope to inspire courage and resilience in others with these problems. I post and publish what I feel, no matter what mood or state of mind I'm in, but I always do my best to keep things positive. I admire people who maintain a positive attitude even when they're having bad days. We all have our battles, but that doesn't mean we have bad lives. A negative mindset will keep you from having a good life. The world suffers a lot due to the silence of good people. Keep going! Keep hope and faith alive! Everyone's struggles are real, and this is why I support talking about mental health.

Today I endured my most symptom-filled morning in months if not years. I have severe schizophrenia. It's all in my mind, of course, and you could say my mind is "diseased." But it's not as if I can return it to the brain exchange!

My favorite band is Duran Duran, and today I finally decided to take a break from listening to their song "Too Close to the Sun" on repeat, while chain smoking and taking in a ton of fluids. My projected lifespan has been shortened by 30 years, and I just turned 40 in January, so I'm working hard to leave a legacy of what I hope is brilliant art, as that is the gift I was born with. It has been a blessing. Thank God, I lost the capacity for off-the-charts IQ as my health has declined. Instead, I realize that the point is to live in the moment. Right now, I am playing "Too Close to the Sun" on my iPhone, and it's not saving my life, but it does soothe my mind. It's what I have but also what I need. In a way, it's *what* I am, if that makes sense; it is a temporary *relief* from the chaos in my mind. Right *now,* I feel one thing: *relief.* Thank you, Lord God.

I am crying now, alone, out of bittersweet joy as I work on my novel. I realize now that it is this, not my *Alibiography*, that will be my legacy. It is called *When We Were Invincible*. I originally wrote it in 1995, during the summer between my senior year of high school and freshman year of college. There is a scene in which the main character is captivated by a portrait of Christ on the Baltic Sea, and he hears Him saying, "How could you have forgotten me?" He comes of age shortly afterward.

And that's what has happened since I wrote the book. I forgot about God. He won't cure me, but He has been there all this time for me. I'm crying tears of bittersweet joy. I remember Him. I also forget at times. I understand, however, and I feel relieved right now. As Simon Le Bon says, "All you need is now." It's a good line, so naturally it's the title of the track and the album. Amen.

Last night, I decided to express myself using one of my many creative outlets, podcasting. The theme for the cast came to me straight away: "When Things Get Tough in Life." As it turned out, I could also have gone with the title "Stigma." I'm not particularly proud of the cast's content. It was one of two I've been unhappy with in the roughly 200 or so episodes I've made for a rather wide audience. My audience members are primarily people seeking self-help, motivation, and inspiration. They are likely the reason I'm here, as they give my life purpose, no matter how or where I share my unconditional love with those who need it most. Sometimes I even just visualize love and light and simply send it spiritually.

Of course, I've felt cornered and victimized before too. To be frank, I don't feel such things often. I vent verbally, and now I'm writing through the morning. I feel as if what I write is channeled through me from some divine entity. I tend, in my healing process, to shy away from topics like religion, government, and conspiracies, as I've learned that these subjects make me susceptible to delusional thinking, which could eventually lead me to experience a schizophrenic break from reality—something that hasn't happened to me in years.

I have learned that when people are rude they are revealing who they are, not who I am, so I do my best not to take it personally. I have learned when everything seems to be going wrong to take a minute and remind myself of everything going right and not to dwell on those who let me down but instead cherish those who lift me up.

I prayed this morning. I have not done so in years. I said, "Lord, today I ask that you bathe those who live in pain in the river of your healing. Amen." I am proud of this because it put my mind at ease. Positivity always wins, as do love and gratitude. These truths escape me at times, but I believe they are part of why I continue to survive, struggling, not suffering, through the minefield—the deep darkness and confusion—that is schizophrenia.

Perhaps I am stronger than I think. Perhaps I am even afraid of my strength and turn it against myself, thus making myself weaker, making myself insecure, and making myself feel guilty. Perhaps I am most afraid of God's strength in me. Perhaps I would rather be guilty and weaker than strong in Him whom I cannot understand.

This whole thought process began recently when I learned I was nearing the end of my struggle. I confronted my father over all the harm he has caused over the past several decades. It has been a challenge, to say the least, but I am proud I spoke my mind to my father. I felt it was a necessary part of my healing process.

As they say, sometimes you have to be your own hero.

This day is brand new. This moment is fresh and clean. The future is a blank canvas waiting to receive the lives we will create. Life is full of twists and turns that often derail the best of souls. Resolve in this moment to continue your journey by honoring the gifts God has given you. If you have fallen off the path, decide to reestablish that connection to whatever fills your heart with gladness. It is never too late to realize your soul's purpose. Do not let "time" fool you into a state of despair. You have the ability to reunite with your true self.

But the question is how?

By embracing all your experiences (yes, even the bad ones), you can strengthen yourself for the journey and ensure that this time there will be a better outcome. Appreciate the difficult times, for they often put your life back on track. Appreciate what you've set in motion, while taking your mind, heart, and soul to the next level of participation. Appreciate the day in the moment. Dwelling in the past makes it difficult to build your future. If you have pushed the proverbial boulder uphill without a struggle, appreciate your own tenacity. If you have tried for a long time to push that same boulder uphill and still haven't succeeded, examine the worth of the boulder, not your own.

Sometimes it's better to let go, allowing the boulder to roll back down the hill and find someone else to push it. This frees you to travel up the hill with ease alone. Fill your moments with expectations, for when you reach the top of the hill there will be unlimited opportunity. You might find that the boulder wasn't necessary at all and that the important moment was your feeling of freedom.

Appreciate that feeling.

I have contemplated many things recently, and there are a few thoughts I feel are worth sharing. I collect such thoughts and place them in what I call my "mental toolbox" or "mental first-aid kit." This works for me.

Every time I get upset about something, I ask myself whether, if I were to die tomorrow, it would have been worth wasting my time being angry about. I let that sink in. Today will never come again. Be a blessing; be a friend; encourage someone; take the time to care and let your words heal, not wound.

"The strongest people are not those who show strength in front of us, but those who fight and win battles we know nothing about."
—Anon

I feel better and stronger now as I await my end. I am strong enough to carry the world on my shoulders. I am stronger than the challenges I face.

So I smile.

And my smile might be worth a thousand words, but sometimes, it seems, its value is even greater. A simple smile creates its own silent message. In many cases, a smile takes on a specific meaning because of the surroundings or context in which it occurs. As a popular saying goes, "Just because a person is always smiling doesn't mean he has no problems. But the smile shows he has the ability to overcome those problems."

And, in closing, I'll leave you with something I once wrote: "How simple it is to acknowledge that all the worry in the world can't control the future. How simple it is to see that we can only be happy now and that there will never be a time that isn't now."
—Jonathan Harnisch, *Jonathan Harnisch: An Alibiography*.

Writing Therapy: Easy Does It

Let's get the facts straight up front to avoid any confusion later. I am a person first, a human being, just like anyone else. Maybe a little different, that's all. Years ago, I publicly disclosed my diagnoses with comorbid schizoaffective disorder, post-traumatic stress disorder, personality disorder NOS (not otherwise specified), and Tourette's syndrome. One might argue that I have been dealt quite a handful of cards and put through the wringer. Maybe it's just the luck of the draw, or maybe it's not luck at all. But some time ago, when I felt internally trapped and suffocated—hiding all my inner demons (as I call them) while also secretly writing about them—*it* simply grabbed hold of me, and boy did it grab hold.

I made seven suicide attempts and had over 30 hospitalizations and rehabilitation stints within a decade. Then, one day, I just made a choice. It felt like the sun smacked my face, allowing my mind, my experiences, and my altered sense of reality to burn, twist, deform, and coil. I am referring to a metamorphosis that had taken place inside me.

I looked into the mirror where everything came alivealizations and rehabilitation stints within a decade. Then, one day, I just made a choicw, I no longer saw impossibility in the mirror. My imagination ignited once again. I kept staring at my reflection. My delusions of grandeur formed a shape of their own in my reflection—in my double reality.

Within the depths of my mind and psyche my imagination began to dream while awake. In short, the metamorphosis occurring inside caused me to begin my mission, excavating all that I had kept buried inside for far too long and letting go of my secret exhaustion that came from suffocating the truth. My truth.

I opened up, raw and unabashed, facing perhaps my hugest fear. I went public with my mental health conditions. One morning, I awakened for the day at midnight and was unable to think clearly, concentrate, or remember much of anything. I dove into my art, my work, my life purpose of productivity, but I couldn't concentrate. Growing more and more upset with myself, I felt a very familiar stinging sense of shame and disapproval. My thoughts, my executive function deficit, were askew along with my condition. I know, this may, rather sound awkward. Ithaps my hugest fear. I went public with my mental health conditions. One morning, I awakened for the day at midnight and was unable to think clearly, concentrate, or rememy morning writing session had gone awry, at least at first.

This is now a part of my regular morning writing sessions.

My concentration had been thrown off, and an overload of stimuli within the silence of my home office frustrated me. I took a hot shower to ground myself, which often does the trick, and then returned to writing. At this point, the original thesis or subject of my words shifted with my thoughts, and that suited me just fine.

Earlier I had been overcome and irritated beyond belieff stimuli within the silence of my home office fy my role as an artist, creating, for example, my latest novel _Jonathan Harnisch: An Alibiography_, my masterpiece. However, the purpose of my sitting at my desk began to metamorphose on its own. That is one thing I love about writing and writing therapy—how it helps me. It keeps things simple, and it helps my thinking become clearer.

Being a mainstream literary author is known to be 50 percent writing and 50 percent marketing, and it was the business aspect, the marketing, that ripped at my soul. At least that was how I felt. I felt defeated. While writing therapy is a tool I take quite seriously—and so perhaps I was not upset with the onslaught of internal difficulties [Editor's Note: Perhaps rephrase? I am not quite sure of intended meaning here.]—my goal of being on the bestseller list no longer matters. That is not why I write. I write for therapy. That is why I keep fighting my mental health condition, my mind, every single day, as I attempt to overcome the demons, the delusions, and the distractions.

Perhaps that morning my cognitive behavioral therapist would have reminded me that the mind plays tricks and that we all suffer in some way from cognitive distortions. He would also have told me how cognitive distortions and living with mental illness take their toll on interpersonal relationships. After all, I believe we are all in the same boat in many ways, and so it comes down to something very clichéd and yet entirely true.

We all have problems, but let's not kid ourselves! It's how we deal with them that makes the difference. I ponder on what the difference is. In my question, I see the answer. I see my self-confident smile once again. Relationships with family and friends have faded and deteriorated in my world, but then just the opposite occurs, sometimes at the drop of a hat. I am grateful for living on a mental roller coaster and not a merry-go-round.

My illnesses make me unusual, as I have said. Sometimes I think we all need to give ourselves a time-out to be alone and figure some things out. Usually, we can see a problem in a new way when we focus our eyes on a new place. That's what the past hour has taught me. It's good. Good enough.

Realistically, things may not be as bad as they seem. Sometimes another perspective on distressing matters can help. I see it as my task, perhaps our collective task, to be resilient even if some days we just have to be there for ourselves when we are feeling alone in the enterprise. We move on. There's no way around it. I ask myself now if I feel okay, and the smile is back. Thank goodness.

One final note. I've often doubted my abilities and my perception of my reality, as I feel myself withdraw inside and lose hope of coming back to myself with any peace of mind. The future— that's not where I am; I'm right here in the now.

Katherine Hepburn once said, "If you obey all the rules, you miss all the fun."

I apply that to writing and writing therapy!

The End